DOWN EAST SCHOONERS AND SHIPMASTERS

DOWN EAST SCHOONERS AND SHIPMASTERS

INGRID GRENON

THE History PRESS

Published by The History Press
Charleston, SC 29403
www.historypress.net

Front cover: The fully rigged *Great Admiral. Courtesy of the Penobscot Marine Museum.*
Back cover: Images courtesy of the Library of Congress.

First published 2012

Manufactured in the United States

ISBN 978.1.60949.514.5

Library of Congress CIP data applied for.

To my ancestors Thomas Richardson and Daniel Gott, who were among the very first Europeans to settle on Mount Desert Island in 1768, and also to my native ancestors who resided in the province known as Maine long before any Europeans appeared.

CONTENTS

ACKNOWLEDGEMENTS

From the Hancock Historical Society, I wish to thank Bertha Smith, Jim Singletary and especially Lois Crabtree Johnson for all her time and endless photocopying, as well as the many wonderful ideas she had for this book.

I wish to thank Ann Benson, Tim Garrity and Deb DeForest from the Mount Desert Historical Society for their time and effort.

I am most grateful for the help of my distant cousin Ralph Stanley and his wife, Marion, from Southeast Harbor on Mount Desert Island.

I owe a debt of gratitude to Cipperly Good, Ben Fuller, Don Garrold and photo archivist Kevin Johnson from the Penobscot Marine Museum in Searsport for allowing me to peruse the Foss Collection and especially for finding the log of the *Edna Hoyt* for me.

I would like to thank marine photographer Craig Milner for helping with the color pictures and editor Whitney Tarella for her invaluable support.

Finally, I wish to thank the crew of the schooner *Lewis R. French* for allowing me to take a few turns at the helm.

Introduction

BLOOD, SEA AND EARTH

My last book, *Lost Maine Coastal Schooners: From Glory Days to Ghost Ships* (The History Press, 2010), was the product of a most unusual circumstance. From out of nowhere, at nearly a half century of age, I became obsessed with Maine schooners. An avid equestrian and professional horsewoman for thirty years, I set aside my boots and spurs and began to research Maine maritime history. I recalled my fascination with the old beached Wiscasset Schooners that I had first seen as a small child going home from a clambake in Boothbay. I begged my parents to stop so that I could see the vessels more closely. Many a child growing up in Maine must have seen the old wrecks on numerous occasions, but my fascination never waned. I remembered that my great-great-great-grandfather Captain William Peachey, who was born on Mount Desert Island in 1805, was a master of schooners. Next, I began to hear the sound of the ocean and seemed to intuitively know what it was like to be on a sailing vessel—although I had never sailed in my life. I seemed to have a familiarity with nautical terminology that I had no conscious recollection of ever hearing before.

After the publication of *Lost Maine Coastal Schooners*, I thought it was over; I believed my sudden and impassioned fascination with Down East schooners and Maine history had ended and that I could go back to riding and training horses, enjoying a brisk morning canter on a favorite equine without being distracted by thoughts of sailing vessels and such. But I was wrong; it had not ended. In fact, it had only begun.

Mount Desert Island called to me just as the island of Bali Ha'i called to Lieutenant Cable in Rogers and Hammerstein's *South Pacific*. I could not get it out of my mind. I remembered that I had ancestors who were among the first to settle Mount Desert Island in the eighteenth century. I wondered if that was part of what was happening.

Last summer, I felt compelled to book passage on the nineteenth-century coasting schooner *Lewis R. French*. I stood on the schooner's deck one evening, watching the sun slowly set just beyond the bowsprit of the majestic vessel, wondering what this obsession with maritime history was all about. We were anchored off Stonington Harbor, where my ancestor had undoubtedly stood at anchor many times in his schooners. How had I become such an unlikely passenger aboard this vessel? I stood watching the sun set; orange, pink, yellow and gold beams extended from the horizon and illuminated the sea around the old schooner. The kerosene lanterns hung in the rigging were casting an eerie glow as present turned into past and past into present, until it was difficult to discern one from the other. And then the answer seemed to appear. At that moment, I thought I heard a voice whisper into my ear, and it seemed to say, "Blood, sea and earth."

Did I really hear that or did I imagine it? I don't know what place parapsychologist Carl Jung's term *synchronicity* has in history books, but many strange "meaningful coincidences" began to occur. Interestingly, I found that the man who built the *Lewis R. French*, and after whom the vessel was named in 1871, was a cousin to an ancestor of mine. I also learned during an initial facet of my research that the shipmaster about whom I write in this book, Captain Harold Foss, was also a distant cousin. As I proceeded with my research, I discovered that many of the people I was meeting were connected to me through blood ties that went back hundreds of years. These are only a few examples of a myriad of occurrences with which I will not tire the reader. It certainly seems, however, that once we are linked by blood, sea and earth we remain so throughout the centuries.

The focus of this history book is people. Some of them have had a tremendous impact on the Maine we see today and some almost no impact at all. Many folks, if not for this book, would likely have long since passed into the realm of the forgotten; I have tried to wake them from their undusted sepulchers and give them a voice. Many others, however, have irrevocably changed the course of history, and their stories have been told countless times before this.

There have been many histories published related to Mount Desert Island, but the histories of the town of Hancock are relatively scant. Many of the stories I have chosen to place in this history aren't well known, and that is why I have selected them. For a more complete history of Mount Desert Island, the reader has many choices. This book, however, is unique and contains information not found in any other account of the region. In addition, it focuses on the strong blood ties the people of coastal Maine have with the sea—ties that still bind, unbelievably, into the present day.

I find it difficult to tell the history of a place and not include the people who were native to the region. The European explorers and colonists literally invaded the American continent beginning in the sixteenth century. They took what they wanted with little or no regard for the native people, as if it was their right to disperse and eliminate an entire civilization. I am descended from *both* the English colonists and the native Wabanaki and without either would cease to exist. I have tried to represent each race equitably and tell their stories as accurately as possible.

I am tied to Maine through birth and maybe something else. Perhaps we are all stained to some extent with some otherworldly residue that won't fade with the passing of the centuries. If so, then one day our past might be reawakened and history will become more than just something we read in books.

A TRAVELER IN TIME

Standing on the fog-shrouded deck of the two-masted Maine-built schooner *Lewis R. French*, it was difficult to determine exactly what century it was. The sea suddenly became curiously silent and calm—dead calm. Then a ghostly form came slowly into view, materializing only about two hundred feet off the *French*'s starboard rail. It was the schooner *Stephen Taber*. She appeared as an image from another era, a traveler in time. Unbelievably, it was June 18, 2011, and the two schooners, both built in 1871, were celebrating the 140th anniversary of their launching. Another schooner, the three-masted *Victory Chimes*, launched in 1900, also came into view just beyond the *Taber*.

"Here comes the *Victory Chimes*," Garth Wells, master of the *Lewis R. French*, announced to the passengers he had taken on for that special day. "She's three-masted and a different class of ship altogether."

Turning to look, I could make out a large schooner silently approaching our vessel, about five hundred feet off the stern. I couldn't quite tell, in the heavy fog, if there were topmasts.

"Is she baldheaded?" I asked. A baldheaded schooner has no topsails.

"Yup, she's bald," Captain Wells replied, matter-of-factly.

Captain Wells looked like a Yankee skipper with his reddish-brown hair and long beard.

Not originally a Maine schooner, the *Victory Chimes* was launched at the turn of the last century in Delaware as the *Edwin & Maude* and was used to transport lumber. Surviving two world wars, U-boats and the ravages of a mechanized world, she began taking on passengers after the Second World War. In 1954, she moved to Maine and was renamed *Victory Chimes*. In 1997, she was declared a historic landmark. In 2003, the people of Maine voted to put her image on their state quarter.

The schooner *Stephen Taber* was built in Long Island, New York, in 1871 and hauled brick, coal, lumber, oysters and other cargoes. In 1936, she came Down East to haul lumber on the Penobscot Bay, where she still sails today. The *Taber* has carried passengers since 1946 and became a historic landmark in 1992.

The *Lewis R. French* was launched in April 1871 in Christmas Cove, Maine, located just northeast of Boothbay Harbor. She carried three thousand square feet of sail and hauled the usual cargoes, including bricks, lumber, cordwood, granite, fish, lime, Christmas trees and even canned sardines. In 1905, the *French* was sold and moved to Mount Desert Island, which was her home port until 1924, when she moved to Bucks Harbor and then Lubec, Maine. In 1973, with nothing else to do, worn out and sitting idle, the *French* was painstakingly restored to her original condition and began taking on passengers. The *Lewis R. French* became a historic landmark in 1992.

Leaning against the windlass at the schooner's bow, Amber, a crew member, slowly cranked the foghorn, which consisted of a black box with a handle on the side. The words "Sch. M. Ford, Rockland" were painted on top of the wooden case, which was only about eighteen inches long but emitted quite a substantial bellow.

"That looks old," I remarked, standing at the bow myself, looking out into the dusky gloom that had fallen like a shroud around the vessel and through which I could see nothing.

"It's an antique," Amber replied, smiling. "Apparently, it belonged to the schooner named *M. Ford*, but it's ours now. It's from the same time period as our ship."

"Where ever did you find it?" I asked.

"Would you believe we got it at a yard sale in Rockland?"

"It's amazing these things are still around," I answered. "Who would ever have imagined that it would be put to work again, on another nineteenth-century schooner in the year 2011?"

Silently, I surveyed the passengers who accompanied me on that morning's sail. Since the participants were restricted to twenty and the

The schooner *Stephen Taber*, built in 1871, was shrouded in fog on June 18, 2011. *Photo ©Craig S. Milner.*

reservations were only available from limited sources, it certainly seemed to be an exclusive group. There were many members of the Maine Maritime Museum, a marine journalist and myself. It seemed unfortunate that there would be so many who would never have the opportunity to sail on a nineteenth-century vessel.

The fog, which had descended on Penobscot Bay, lingered amidst these windjammers just before they left the dock in Rockland, obscuring all signs of the modern world, and only began to lift as we returned to the harbor. It would seem that even Mother Nature wanted to celebrate the schooners' 140 years of stalwart resistance to change by temporarily erasing all evidence of the twenty-first century on that special day. Perhaps it is no coincidence that these ships ended up in Maine waters.

The resurrected coasting schooners, representatives of an era long passed, presented me with a considerable opportunity. The view from the sea differs greatly from that of the more traveled inland roadways, and one lucky enough to travel by sailing vessel can get a glimpse of a part of Maine that is untouched by time. Unable to resist this temptation, I booked a four-day passage on the *Lewis R. French*.

It was a warm day in mid-August when I headed Down East to the Penobscot Bay region in coastal Maine, where the schooner *French* was lying at her home port of Camden. Those indigenous to the area knew it as *Megunticook*, meaning "place of great sea swells." According to George Varney in his 1886 *Gazetteer of the State of Maine*, "Megunticook affords one of the noblest of marine prospects, embracing Penobscot Bay with its islands, Mount Desert at the east, and a vast sweep of the ocean on the south-east."

The first English settlers came to the area after the end of the French and Indian Wars; James Richards was the first in 1769. In 1791, the Massachusetts General Court incorporated Megunticook Plantation as Camden. The "place of great sea swells" can also be considered to be a place of great shipbuilding. By the latter part of the nineteenth century, there were many mills, factories and shipyards in Camden. In August 1900, the Holly M. Bean Shipyard launched the very first six-masted schooner, the *George W. Wells*, depriving the famed Percy and Small Shipyard in Bath of the honor. Percy and Small launched the *Eleanor A. Percy* on October 10. Camden certainly earned its place as a shipbuilding center and schooner town.

Arriving in Camden a few hours before sunset allowed me to get a feel of the picturesque old coastal village, touted today as one of the most charming in Maine. Visitors to Camden cannot miss the traditional New England–style white church situated in the middle of town, its immense steeple overlooking the harbor as a sentry would his charge. Across from the harbor is the park, with its mélange of grass and granite and two small brick structures, each sporting slate roofs and old weather vanes. Illuminated by a streetlamp, one weather vane depicted a three-masted brig and spun around slowly in the evening breeze, casting eerie shadows in the dim light.

I was to board the vessel that night, before we sailed. I noticed the tide had all but gone out as I made my way to the schooner *French* via the long wooden plank wharf. There at the end, she rested on her tether, restlessly rising and falling in cadence with the ebb and flow of the tide. Beside the *French* there was another windjammer; the name displayed on her stern was *Mary Day*. I caught the familiar scent of the ocean, and it evoked many childhood memories of growing up in proximity to the sea, pervading until it became so familiar that I no longer noticed it. Coming alongside the *French*,

I saw the rope ladder attached to the side of the ship, which moved slowly back and forth between sea and wharf. I wondered if a misstep would land either me or my gear in the seawater if I wasn't careful.

The crew welcomed me aboard, and the captain's wife, Jenny, smiled and pointed to the companionway that led to my quarters. There was a sign advising the traveler to "go down backward," as the narrow ladder leading below deck would certainly be difficult to navigate any other way. I stowed my sea bag under the bunk and spied my surroundings; above my berth there was a small window that overlooked the starboard deck, and beside the door there was a small mirror and a few hooks. There was barely enough room to turn around. I was surprised at how I quickly became accustomed to my surroundings.

The next day, I awoke to peer through the window in my cabin, and looking up through the morning fog I could see the ratlines and spars of the schooner *Mary Day* beside us. For a moment I wondered how the picture might differ if I were in a previous century but could think of nothing.

We got underway that morning, after the firewood for the woodstove and the provisions were loaded. I attempted to raise the foresail, which is something that looks a whole lot easier than it really is. I don't think I was really very much help, and luckily the first mate came over and took over the ropes. It became easy to imagine how much hard work it must have taken to keep a sailing vessel going a century or two ago, and I had barely got a taste of it.

Once the mainsail, main topsail, foresail and jibs were set, the schooner really began to pick up speed. The large sails billowed a bit, and the ship swayed and vibrated just a tad as she sped through the salt water en route to North Haven. Once we were out on the ocean, the freedom seemed immeasurable, and it was as if we were all being ushered into a completely different realm.

"Look off the port rail!" I heard somebody exclaim. Turning to see what the commotion was about, I saw a few porpoises swimming alongside the schooner. Not long afterward, we sailed past harbor seals basking on a rocky ledge.

Standing on the deck, I watched as the tall masts seemingly pierced the bright blue sky and billowing white clouds. The gentle sway of the ship in the sea, the smell of the fresh ocean air and the sound of the salt water washing up against the bow became almost hypnotic. I looked aloft and watched the colorful flags fixed high atop the masts and on the running rigging fluttering in the breeze. This could have been a scene from another century, I thought, until a closer look revealed that one of the flags was imprinted with the words "Boston Red Sox."

Looking aft, I saw the captain and the mate embroiled in conversation at the helm and wanted to get a closer look at the operation. It certainly looked simple: turn the wheel one way and then another. Check out the scenery.

"Go ahead," Captain Wells said, walking away from the helm. "Take the wheel."

"Really?"

"Really," the captain said, smiling. "Pick out a point in the distance, a landmark that will be easy for you to see," he told me. Then, pointing toward a white blur in the distance, he added, "Like that lighthousc out there on Vinalhaven. Head toward that."

The ship's wheel, of course, controlled the large wooden rudder beneath the stern of the vessel. One needed to expel only a moderate amount of effort to move the wheel back and forth, and the degree of attention required was dependent on the movements of the wind. The ship seemed to respond a bit sluggishly to the turn of the wheel, at least for somebody used to driving a twenty-first-century automobile.

"See that big red buoy ahead?" Captain Wells asked, pointing over the port rail. "Keep away from that," he explained. "It's a ledge only a few feet below the surface. Give her plenty of room to clear it."

"Oh no," I exclaimed, suddenly remembering the past. "Perhaps you should take the wheel back. My ancestor was master of a schooner just like this one, the *General Meade*, and he ran her up onto the Green Island ledge in Casco Bay during a storm in December 1876," I explained. "She was loaded with granite from Vinalhaven for Boston, and I think he tried to make it into Portland Harbor…but the vessel was lost in the storm."

"Don't worry," Garth Wells replied, smiling as he lifted a piece of canvas off what appeared to be a storage compartment near the helm. "Your ancestor didn't have this."

What the captain revealed to me was a state-of-the-art GPS, cleverly hidden.

"How any of those early shipmasters managed to navigate these waters was a miracle," he admitted.

"Where are we?" I asked.

"They call this the Deer Island Thoroughfare," he replied.

It was great. I carefully moved the wheel first one way and then another, keeping my reference point in sight. I tried to keep the bowsprit facing the lighthouse for the most part, occasionally allowing it to drift away so that I could experience the thrill of actually turning the vessel. Making the moderate adjustment under sail with a breeze, I spun the wheel around, and moments later the schooner responded, bowsprit gently bobbing up and down, pointing in the new direction. I could feel the immense sails filling with wind and the effect that had on altering the course.

After what seemed like quite a while, I realized there was something wrong.

"Have you got any steerageway?" the captain inquired.

"No."

"You're sailing too close to the wind. You'll have to change your landmark now," he said, pointing aloft. "You can tell by watching the flags what direction the wind is blowing."

Not very long afterward the wind stopped completely.

"What should I do?" I asked, noticing the schooner was just drifting with the current.

Garth Wells laughed. "Nothing we can do but sit here and wait."

"Just walk away?" I asked.

"Turn the wheel all the way to one side," Captain Wells said, slowly spinning the wheel all the way around to starboard. "That will bring the rudder as far over as it can go. Then bring the wheel back three full turns, and it should be right in the middle, pointed straight ahead. That way," he added, "she won't do anything bad if a breeze suddenly comes up."

When the breeze did eventually appear, the captain took advantage of it and sailed the vessel for hours, even throughout much of the evening. Tired after a full day, I retired to my quarters below, thankful that I had that luxury.

I found it appropriate to bring, as reading material while traveling on the schooner, an 1895 edition of Richard Henry Dana's *Two Years Before the Mast.* The small, hardcover volume was in pretty good condition, and despite some discolored pages, it was hard to believe that it was over a century old.

With the exception of the battery-powered reading lamp that hung over the narrow bunk below deck on the old schooner, the rest of my cabin seemed to remain free from the influences of the twenty-first, or even the twentieth, century. Deep inside the vessel, I was nestled amongst the ancient timbers that formed the ship's inner structure, able to touch the hand-hewn beams crafted by nineteenth-century shipbuilders.

As the ocean tossed the ship back and forth, I could hear the seas washing up against the wooden hull beside my berth on the schooner. It might sound strange, but I found the swaying back and forth of the ship comforting, as if Mother Nature were rocking the cradle. I was thankful that Captain Wells had decided to take advantage of a brisk evening wind and sail at night. Although it was August, it was after dark, and I was glad to have a woolen blanket to safeguard against the evening chill.

It certainly seemed to be a good night for reading, I thought, reaching again for Dana's faded terra cotta–colored volume. I interrupted my reading only occasionally, stopping to watch, in the shadows, a scrimshaw pendant slowly swing back and forth on a hook next to an antique mirror. Within my present surroundings aboard the schooner, it wasn't difficult to imagine what Mr. Dana described in his exposé about life on a nineteenth-century sailing vessel.

On the next morning, I awoke abruptly to the thunderous sound of the anchor chains being hauled up through the cathead as men worked the windlass. The first mate, Ryan, wasted no opportunity to evoke a period "feel" to the undertaking. His measured shouts of "Heave ho!" rang throughout the vessel, easily heard below deck in my cabin.

That day began with a light rain that would become constant and heavy by midday, with strong winds. Captain Wells donned a yellow rain slicker with a wide-brimmed hat and stood at the helm exposed to the weather, water dripping down over his hands and face. The ship's wheel appeared to be wet and cold.

"Would you like to take another turn at the helm, or is the weather too foul for you?" Captain Wells asked, noticing me climbing up onto the poop deck.

"Not too foul. I'll take the wheel, it's nice out here," I answered. I wasn't being completely truthful, however, and probably would have preferred to go below with a hot cup of coffee, but I was determined to get some authentic experience aboard the nineteenth-century vessel.

"OK, let's get some rain gear on you," he said, going below to find me a slicker and a hat.

I found that despite the protective clothing, it was still challenging to remain above deck at the wheel. I stood at the helm with the wind-swept rain blowing onto my face and my cold, wet hands fixed on the iron wheel. I did my best to guide the old craft along on her way, straining to make out landmarks through the driving rain. I shivered for over an hour, standing out on the deck of the schooner in the cool August rain, trying to get a feel for what it might have been like a century earlier. I imagined the same job in January, with rough seas and everything on the schooner covered in ice, including me. I was beginning to appreciate the phrase "wooden ships and iron men," as I could not even endure a summer rain.

Fortunately, the afternoon brought with it some clearing, and by the time sunset was upon us, the sky shone brilliantly with many hues of orange, pink, yellow and red. The mountains rising on the mainland appeared blue against the backdrop of the setting sun, which reflected its golden rays across the now calm ocean.

"Let go the anchor!" Captain Wells shouted from somewhere aft.

"Letting go the anchor!" the mate repeated from the bow of the schooner, after which ensued a splash and then the sound of chains unraveling. Afterward, the mate lit the kerosene lanterns and placed them in the rigging.

"Where are we?" I asked, noticing there were no signs of human handiwork anywhere. We seemed to be at some remote location, surrounded by uninhabited islands.

"They call this Merchants' Row," Captain Wells, standing nearby, answered. "It's just a group of islands lying between Deer Isle and Isle au Haut. We're outside Stonington Harbor tonight," he added, pointing. The far-off village of Stonington was vaguely apparent due to its lights.

The stars shone incredibly bright, and the sky was clear. Feeling a cool breeze creep aboard the old ship, I buttoned my shirt and turned up the collar. The lamps in the rigging imparted an "other-era" feel that was difficult to resist, especially when I looked aloft and saw the fore-topmast silhouetted against the rising moon. The sea was calm, and I heard only the occasional creak of the rigging. I noticed the whir of the passing of time seemed to have slowed significantly. I was certain the early visitors to this part of Maine, back in the sixteenth and seventeenth centuries, must have anchored here amongst these islands as well. I wondered what they thought of the jagged, rock-strewn coastline. Although extremely hazardous to vessels of any kind, its rugged beauty is unsurpassed. I wondered what brought them here, many miles away from their own civilized countries and into unknown seas.

EARLY VISITORS—LOOKING FOR NORUMBEGA

The search for Xanadu, Eden, Norumbega or cities made of gold is a quest that has enchanted people from the very beginnings of civilization. Early explorers of the New World really had exploitation on their minds more than exploration. The European discoverers of Maine were no different. They were simply looking for a shortcut or passage through the landmass that would take them quickly to Asia and India and the lucrative spice trade there. It was believed that what is now the American continent was simply a narrow strip of land dividing the Atlantic and Pacific Oceans. Rumors of cities dripping with gold also abounded. In sixteenth-century Europe, there was fierce competition to see which nation would be the first to find the passage to the Pacific and the gold. In *Bryant's Popular History of the United States*, published in 1876, the authors described Norumbega as "the name by which Maine was earliest known in England."

Giovanni da Verrazzano was an Italian navigator sailing for Francis I of France who, in 1524, visited Maine waters during his search for both the passage to the Orient and the fabled golden city of Norumbega. Before reaching Maine, Verrazzano sailed along the Atlantic coast, taking many liberties and claiming all that he saw for the king of France. In his "Letter to King Francis in 1524," Verrazzano described meeting natives on the mainland, specifically an old woman and what appeared to be her daughter and grandson:

> *We took the boy from the old woman to carry back to France, and we wanted to take the young woman, who was very beautiful and tall, but it was impossible to take her to the sea because of the loud cries she uttered.*

Near what is now Casco Bay, Verrazzano met with some unfriendly natives, and this confrontation led him to call Maine "Land of Bad People." Later in his "Letter to King Francis," Verrazzano described an incident that occurred while his crew traded with the Casco Bay Indians:

> *We found no courtesy in them, and when we had nothing more to exchange and left them, the men made all the signs of scorn and shame that any brute creature would make such as showing their buttocks and laughing.*

As Verrazzano moved farther up the coast to the northeast, his impression of the indigenous peoples did not change. The twenty-first-century reader who knows his history may very well imagine that these natives in sixteenth-century Maine had the right idea. Historian and author Samuel Eliot Morison, in his book *The European Discovery of America*, postulates that the Maine natives' (or Wabanaki) bad attitude toward the Europeans suggests that the Maine coast had been raided previously for slaves.

In 1527, Verrazzano made another visit to the New World, believing the elusive passage to the Orient was farther south than he had gone on the previous journeys. In 1528, after exploring Florida, the Bahamas and the Lesser Antilles, Verrazzano went ashore on Guadeloupe, where he was captured by Carib Indians, cut into pieces and eaten.

During much of the sixteenth century, the Spanish were vying with the French for rights to the New World. In 1525, Estevan Gomes, a Portuguese navigator loyal to Charles V of Spain, visited the coast of Maine, including Mount Desert Island, while looking for passage to Asia. He was also keeping an eye open for the fabled city of Norumbega. At first, he believed the Penobscot River to be the passage to the Pacific, and he named it the Rio de las Gamas, or River of the Deer, and followed it to present-day Bangor. Realizing his mistake but not wanting to return empty-handed, he kidnapped some Wabanaki Indians, fifty-eight of whom he sold in Spain as slaves. Interestingly, Gomes sailed with Ferdinand Magellan in 1519 and was captain of the largest vessel in Magellan's fleet, the *San Antonio*, but deserted and returned to Spain due to horrendous weather conditions encountered near what is now the Straight of Magellan. Although imprisoned for mutiny in Spain, Gomes was later freed when his tales of frightful weather and incredibly stormy seas were corroborated by his crew members. It is no surprise that Gomes later returned to the New World looking for his own passage to the Pacific.

After Gomes's exploration of the Northeast, many maps based on his expedition and notes depicted the area he called "Rio de las Gamas" as "Tierra de Norumbega." These maps implied that Norumbega was a city of tremendous wealth, despite Gomes's inscription on his own map of the Penobscot River in which he indicated there was no gold. In 1535, Gomes sailed with others to South America, still looking for silver and gold, and in 1538, having found neither a passage to the Pacific nor precious metals, he was ambushed by Indians near the Paraguay River and killed.

When one studies early Maine history, and especially the origins of the fabled city of Norumbega, one is bound to come across the name of David Ingram. It is generally accepted that Ingram was an English seaman who, in October 1568, was put ashore in Florida by John Hawkins during an expedition that included Francis Drake. Hawkins and Drake were in business together, providing a special commodity to the Spanish colonists in the West Indies. John Hawkins was following the same avocation that had made his father, William, a fortune. John Hawkins's ship, the *Jesus of Lubec*, was a slaver.

In 1567, after years of successful business ventures, Hawkins and Drake left England and again made their way toward Africa, arriving on the eighteenth of November at Cape Verde, where they planned to capture that very lucrative human cargo. The exact number of ships taking part in this journey is not known. Unfortunately for Hawkins and Drake, however, the inhabitants of Cape Verde had other plans. According to Hawkins's own description of this event, in his *The Third Troublesome Voyage Made with the* Jesus of Lubec, *1567–1568*:

> *We landed 150 men, hoping to obtain some Negros, where we got but fewe, and those with great hurt and damage to our men, which chiefly proceeded of their envenomed arrowes: and although in the beginning they seemed to be but small hurts, yet they hardly escaped any that had blood drawen of them, but died in strange sort, with their mouthes shut some tenne days before they died, and after their wounds were whole.*

Moving up the coast of West Africa to Guinea, more events transpired that were of a similar nature, resulting in the death of six men and injuries to forty more. Despite what Hawkins described as many more "troublesome" events, it would seem that he finally managed to abduct between four and five hundred West Africans. With this profitable cargo in the hold of the vessel, Hawkins headed for the New World:

> *We thought it somewhat reasonable to seeke the coast of the West Indies, and there, for our Negros, and our other merchandise, we hoped to obtain, whereof to countervaile our charges with some gains.*

Hawkins and his expedition, after experiencing difficulty selling their "cargo," continued to meet with disaster after disaster. They encountered seasonal storms, were fired on and pursued by Spanish ships and eventually began to suffer from starvation and thirst. With the seriously damaged *Jesus of Lubec*, shorn of some of her yards and masts by Spanish gunfire, Hawkins continued:

> *So thus with many sorrowful hearts we wandred in an unknowen Sea by the space of 14 dayes, till hunger inforced us to seek the land, for hides were thought very good meat, rats, cats, mice and dogs, none escaped that might be gotten, parrats and monkeyes that were had in great price, were thought there very profitable if they served the turne one dinner.*

It must seem unlikely to the reader that any of these incidents could possibly have a thing to do with the history of Maine, but in fact they do. Although one can hardly feel sorry for Hawkins and his retinue, the string of troublesome events that plagued the *Jesus of Lubec* did lead to an interesting facet of early Maine history. Rather than starve, many sailors pleaded to be taken to land. In October 1568, John Hawkins put 114 men ashore in Florida:

> *These hundred men we set a land with all diligence in this little place beforesaid, which being landed, we determined there to take in fresh water, and so with our little remaine of victuals to take the sea.*

Of these grounded sailors, three began walking to the north; they were David Ingram, Richard Brown and Richard Twide. Unbelievably, sometime in 1571, David Ingram arrived in Maine, sailed up the Penobscot River and visited what is now Bangor. He eventually made his way to New Brunswick, Canada, and found passage back to England on a French vessel. Although Ingram's journey is incredible, this extraordinary story does not end here.

Once back in England, David Ingram began to tell his shipmates about the wonders of the New World and detailed his experiences. He talked specifically about the natives of Maine, their strange customs and manner of dress, and he told of a city of gold on the banks of a great river. Not surprisingly, English authorities formally examined Ingram in 1582. Ingram's testimony, as recorded in the original sixteenth-century transcript, reads as follows:

> *Generallye all men weare about there armes dyvers hoopes of gold and silver wch are of good thickness and lykwyse they weare the lyke about the smale of there leggs wch hoopes are garnished wth pearle dyvers of them as bigge as ones thume…the womenne of the countrye gooe apareled wth plats of gold over there bodye much lyke unto an armor…lykewyse about there armes and the smale of there leggs they wear hoopes of gold and silver garnished wth fayer pearle.*

Ingram also tells his examiners that there is "a great aboundance of gold, silver and pearle and of other jewells." He says he has seen pieces of gold as big as his fist in springs and brooks and also that "there be wyld horses of goodly shape but the people of the country have not the use of them." Mr. Ingram claims to have seen all of this in the Maine woods!

Whether Ingram's city of gold on the Penobscot River is a product of actual experience or of something he ingested at local pubs, I'll leave the reader to decide. The fact is that most people believed his tales of uncounted wealth, including Sir Humphrey Gilbert, explorer and member of Parliament. Humphrey Gilbert was father to Raleigh Gilbert, who would become second in command at Popham Colony, the first attempt by the English to colonize Maine in 1607.

Samuel Eliot Morison, in his *Story of Mount Desert Island*, alludes to Norumbega being nothing more than a story concocted by the Wabanaki and told to the first Europeans to visit the Maine coast, likely fishermen who seasonally traveled to the coast of New England. Whatever the origins of the Norumbega legend may have been, it continued to plague the imagination of European entrepreneurs.

It is not my intention to overwhelm the reader by chronicling every European to visit the northeastern portion of the New World, but there is another fellow who did set foot on Maine soil and who sailed into the Penobscot Bay region. Englishman Martin Pring visited the coast of Maine in 1603, supposedly looking for sassafras, which was a lucrative cargo in the seventeenth century. Sassafras was highly regarded for its many curative properties and was sought after during colonial times. Pring, in his original seventeenth-century journal, described his visit to what are now the islands of North Haven and Vinalhaven:

> *We sayled to the South-west end of these Ilands, and there rode with our ships under one of the greatest. One of them we named Foxe Iland* [this island is still known as Fox Island], *because we found those kind of beasts thereon.*

Martin Pring also described the "savages" that he encountered during his stay in the land, stating that they visited with his contingent in groups ranging in size from as few as 10 to as many as 120 at a time. According to Pring, "They did eat Pease and Beanes with our men. Their owne victuals were most of fish."

Pring's description of the savages' manner of dress is quite interesting and certainly worth reproducing:

> *These people in colour are inclined to a swart, tawnie, or Chestnut colour, not by nature but accidentally, and doe weare their haire brayded in foure parts, and trussed up about their heads with a small knot behind: in which haire of theirs they sticke many feathers and toyes for braverie and pleasure. They cover their privities only with a piece of leather drawne betwixt their twists and fastened to their Girdles* [these were made of long snakeskins] *behind and before: where unto they hang their bags of Tobacco. They seeme to bee somewhat jealous of their women, for we saw not past two of them, who weare Aprons of Leather skins before them downe to the knees, and a Beares skinne like an Irish Mantle over one shoulder.*

It is worth mentioning that the Englishman Pring, at this time, referred to Maine as "the Northpart of Virginia," in an area later known as New England. Sir Walter Raleigh is believed to have named the entire area north of Spanish Florida on the East Coast "Virginia" in honor of his queen, Elizabeth I, who was known as the "virgin" queen.

There were so many nations vying for possessions in the New World! It would soon be time for the French to fortify their colonization efforts, which would leave a lasting impression on what is known today as the state of Maine.

ILE DES MONTS DÉSERTS

In 1603, Henry IV of France appointed a nobleman, a Sieur De Monts, as lieutenant general of New France, granting him authority over all lands from present-day Pennsylvania into Canada. It would be De Monts' duty to ensure that the savages were converted to Christianity, to colonize the lands and, most importantly, to search for precious metals. Samuel de Champlain would be De Monts' navigator and guide.

Champlain began his military career in the army of Henry IV in 1587, when he became a quartermaster of cavalry whose responsibilities included the care and feeding of the king's horses. Despite these humble beginnings, it would appear that he was destined for a place in our history books. It was when he was working for De Monts that Champlain stumbled upon Mount Desert Island in 1604, while seeking the fabled golden city of Norumbega, but he seemed less inclined than others to believe that he would actually find it.

Champlain was a different sort of fellow than most of his predecessors, and Francis Parkman, in *Pioneers of France in the New World*, published in 1897, described him as "a Catholic of good family." Parkman further added, "His purse was small, his merit great; and Henry the Fourth out of his own slender revenues had given him a pension to maintain him near his person." William Williamson, in his distinguished *History of the State of Maine*, first published in 1832, described Champlain as "a gentleman of noble birth and of skill in navigation." It soon becomes clear to the reader of these early histories that Samuel de Champlain was highly regarded for both his talent and his integrity.

According to Champlain himself, as noted in J. Franklin Jameson's *Voyages of Samuel de Champlain*, published in 1907, "Sieur de Monts, without losing time, decided to send persons to make discoveries along the coast of Norumbegue; and he intrusted me with this work, which I found very agreeable." On September 2, 1604, when De Monts sent Champlain off to find Norumbega, Champlain reported:

> *In order to execute this commission, I set out from St. Croix* [a French settlement that was located in Maine on the Canadian border] *on the 2d of September with a patache* [a small, narrow boat] *of seventeen or eighteen tons, twelve sailors, and two savages, to serve us as guides to the places with which they were acquainted.*

The expedition was delayed for a few days due to bad weather and dense fog. Then finally, on September 5, after passing "a large number of islands, banks, reefs, and rocks," Champlain nearly lost his ship. "We just escaped being lost on a little rock on a level with the water, which made an opening in our barque near the keel." Afterward, Champlain described his first glimpse of a large island:

> *It is very high, and notched in places, so that there is the appearance to one at sea, as of seven or eight mountains extending along near each other. The summit of the most of them is destitute of trees, as there are only rocks on them. The woods consist of pines, firs, and birches only. I named it Isle des Monts Déserts.*

The next day, while still searching for Norumbega, two canoes rowed by natives came near to the vessel, and Champlain sent out his two "savages" to gain their confidence, but frightened, the natives rowed away. The next day, they returned and "came alongside of our barque and talked with our savages." Champlain, with hopes of enlisting their help in his search for the fabled city, gave them biscuits and tobacco:

> *These savages had come beaver-hunting and to catch fish, some of which they gave us. Having made an alliance with them, they guided us to their*

> *river of Pentegouët* [the Penobscot], *so called by them, where they told us was their captain, named Bessabez, chief of this river. I think this river is that which several pilots and historians call Norumbegue, and which most have described as large and extensive, with very many islands…But that any one has ever entered it there is no evidence, for then they would have described it in another manner…I will accordingly relate truly what I explored and saw, from the beginning as far as I went.*
>
> *In the first place, there are at its entrance several islands distant ten or twelve leagues from the main land, which are in latitude 44°, and 18°40' of the deflection of the magnetic needle. The Isle des Monts Déserts forms one of the extremities of the mouth, on the east; the other is low land, called by the savages Bedabedec* [in the vicinity of today's Rockland and Camden], *to the west of the former, the two being distant from each other nine or ten leagues. Almost midway between these, out in the ocean, there is another island very high and conspicuous, which on this account I have named Isle Haute.*

Champlain, in his writings, certainly inspires confidence in his readers that what he has written is a truthful account and not merely an embellishment to stir the interest of others. His attention to detail is noteworthy, and his descriptions of flora and fauna, as well as the local "savages," are interesting. Champlain gives the reader an invaluable glimpse into the early history of the region as he describes people and events that have long since disappeared and perhaps without his recollections would be lost altogether.

On his trip up the Penobscot River, Champlain made his way near to what is present-day Bangor, Maine. He noted, while on a hunting excursion, that "the oaks here appear as if they were planted for ornament," further adding, "We saw no town, nor village, nor the appearance of there having been one." Champlain did comment on seeing "cabins of the savages" and stated they were not inhabited. He said they were covered with the bark of trees, and the savages seemed to have "no fixed abode."

Certainly seeming well intentioned, Champlain described his attempts to befriend the natives by arranging a meeting with them. "There came some thirty savages," Champlain wrote, "on assurances given them by those who had served us as guides." Eventually, many more natives gathered:

> *There came also to us the same day Bessabez* [the regional chief] *with six canoes. As soon as the savages who were on land saw him coming, they*

all began to sing, dance, and jump, until he had landed. Afterwards they all seated themselves in a circle on the ground, as is their custom, when they wish to celebrate a festivity, or an harangue is to be made. Cabahis, the other chief, arrived a little later with twenty or thirty of his companions, who withdrew one side and greatly enjoyed seeing us, as it was the first time they had seen Christians...Bessabez bade us sit down, and began to smoke with his companions, as they usually do before an address. They presented us with venison and game.

Champlain then told the interpreter to inform the native chiefs that Sieur de Monts had sent him to see them and that he desired their friendship. The chiefs were told that Sieur de Monts would reconcile them with their enemies and inhabit their country in order to show them how to farm and cultivate it, "in order that they might not continue to lead so miserable a life." Certainly it did not occur to Champlain that the lives these natives were leading were far from miserable or that one day the very discovery of their lands would result in the eventual eradication of their culture. We cannot fault Champlain for being a product of his time, as we all are, and it certainly appears to the reader of the journal of his voyages that his intention was well meaning. Champlain dispelled the myth of the fabulous golden city of Norumbega in the following manner:

All these people of Norumbegue are very swarthy, dressed in beaver-skins and other furs, like the Canadian and Souriquois savages, and they have the same mode of life.

The above is an exact statement of all that I have observed respecting not only the coasts and people, but also the river Norumbegue; and there are none of the marvels there which some persons have described.

It may be of some interest to those curious about early Maine history to know of the hardships Champlain and his crew suffered on the Island of St. Croix during the fall and winter of 1604:

The snows began on the 6th of October. On the 3rd of December, we saw ice pass which came from some frozen river. The cold was sharp, more severe than in France, and of much longer duration; and it scarcely rained at all the entire winter. I suppose that is owing to the north and north-west winds

> *passing over high mountains always covered with snow. The latter was from three to four feet deep up to the end of the month of April.*

The snow wasn't the only thing Champlain's crew suffered from on St. Croix Island. Scurvy killed nearly half of the men in his party. Interestingly, in 1535, Jacques Cartier's men had also suffered the same malady while wintering near present-day Quebec, and the natives cured them by making a tea out of evergreen leaves. Champlain wasn't so lucky. Of seventy-nine men, Champlain related, "thirty-five died and more than twenty were on the point of death." In case the twenty-first-century reader does not fully appreciate the effects of scurvy, Champlain described them for us:

> *There were produced, in the mouths of those who had it, great pieces of superfluous and drivelling flesh (causing extensive putrefaction), which got the upperhand to such an extent that scarcely anything but liquid could be taken. Their teeth became very loose, and could be pulled out with the fingers without its causing them pain. The superfluous flesh was often cut out, which caused them to eject much blood through the mouth. Afterwards, a violent pain seized their arms and legs, which remained swollen and very hard, all spotted as if with flea-bites; they could not walk on account of the contraction of the muscles, so that they were almost without strength, and suffered intolerable pains.*

St. Croix Island in Maine became known as "Bone Island" in the eighteenth century after the remains of those in Champlain's party who perished from scurvy were exposed by erosion. In 1969, the skeletons were removed and studied, revealing signs of having been autopsied just as Champlain stated in his journal. According to scientists, this makes Maine the likely site of North America's earliest autopsy.

Champlain, of course, continued to explore the Northeast coast. Sailing as far to the south as Massachusetts, he encountered some resistance from members of the Nauset tribe on Cape Cod and moved northward again to found Quebec City in 1608 and to chart Lake Champlain in 1609. His impact on early Maine history is notable.

Champlain is still spoken of today, unbelievably, in everyday conversation along the coast of Maine. On the coasting schooner *Lewis R. French*, while heading toward the island of North Haven, we passed Fox Island, named by Englishman Martin Pring in 1603. As we approached Pulpit Harbor with a fair breeze upon our canvas, I heard nothing but the sea lapping against the wooden hull of the aged sailing vessel and the mainsail boom traveler occasionally shifting back and forth. It was quite tranquil as we glided past the islands, which appeared like giant granite formations jutting out of the ocean, covered only by a thick blanket of evergreens. The sea, sort of a greenish blue, washed rhythmically against the shore as a warm August breeze tossed my hair. The sun illuminated the granite on shore and cast its reflection in the water. Scenes such as this nearly lulled me into believing that time itself had somehow been turned back.

As we approached Pulpit Rock, at the entrance to Pulpit Harbor, I was suddenly brought back into the present.

"You're the historian," Ryan, first mate on the *French*, exclaimed. "See the osprey nest out on that big rock?" He pointed ahead. "Champlain noted an osprey nest on that same rock back around 1604."

"I guess things just don't change a lot out here," I replied.

"That's called Pulpit Rock," Ryan added. "Look, see the osprey?"

THE JESUITS

In May 1610, François Ravaillac, a Catholic zealot, murdered King Henry IV of France in Paris. King Henry, formerly a Huguenot or French Protestant, had converted to Catholicism, so it is interesting that he was murdered by Ravaillac. The king's coach was actually stuck in traffic, with a hay cart on one side and another carriage obstructing the narrow road, when Ravaillac stabbed him twice between the ribs. According to John Gifford in his *History of France*, published in 1793, the king was particularly vulnerable because, of his two footmen, "one went before to clear the passage, while the other staid behind to tie up his garter." Perhaps if not for the plunging garter, Henry IV might have survived, and history would have taken a different turn. Ravaillac was tortured and drawn and quartered for his act. Let me define this method of execution for the twenty-first-century reader, as it specifically pertains to this incident. While he was still alive, molten lead and boiling oil were poured over Ravaillac's naked body, after which bits of flesh were torn off. Next, he was literally pulled apart by four horses. His execution was more vividly described by John Frost in his *Great Events in Modern History*, published in 1855:

> *He was carried in a cart to Notre Dame, there to ask pardon of the Almighty for the dreadful deed he had committed, and thence taken to Place de Greve, where his right hand was burned from his body by sulpher, his limbs were*

> *torn with pincers, and melted lead, boiling oil, flaming rosin were poured on his wounds. The infliction was long protracted, and the groans and struggles of the culprit are said to have been witnessed with joy by the populace. He was finally attached to four horses, which pulling in opposite directions, at length terminated his existence, by tearing his body to pieces. Fragments of his corpse were then siezed by the excited crowd.*

The king's assassination set in motion a sequence of events that resulted in the establishment of Saint Sauveur, the first Jesuit mission in North America, on Mount Desert Island. Sieur de Monts lost his position as lieutenant general of New France, and his successor, a woman, Antoinette de Pons, Marquise de Guercheville, became the sole proprietor of New France. New France at this time included all of North America. The Marquise de Guercheville was a staunch supporter of the Jesuits, and it was through her effort and financial backing that the mission was established on Mount Desert Island in 1613.

The marquise was noted for a few things, primarily her dedication to her faith and her desire to convert the savages of the New World to Catholicism. She was also the only woman known to have resisted the amorous advances

Henry IV as depicted in the author's 1793 copy of John Gifford's *History of France.*

of King Henry IV. It would seem that King Henry was quite smitten with the attractive marquise—or, more precisely, obsessed with her. According to Gifford, Henry IV's "propensity for play was carried to excess and his passion for the fair sex extreme." Nevertheless, the Marquise de Guercheville stuck to her principles. In his *Pioneers of France in the New World*, Francis Parkman quoted the marquise as saying, "Sire, my rank, perhaps, is not high enough to permit me to be your wife, but my heart is too high to permit me to be your mistress."

History seems to be made up of strange twists of fate. A Spanish knight, skilled in the art of warfare and having a weakness for women, was severely wounded when a cannonball tore through his leg during a battle with France in 1521. During his lengthy recovery, which resulted in lots of rest and time for reflection, he experienced a transformation of sorts. The wounded knight's name was Ignatius of Loyola, who founded the Society of Jesus in 1539. The priests in this order were referred to as Jesuits and were considered an integral facet of the Counter-Reformation, which was the Catholic response to the Protestant Reformation.

In March 1613, as a result of the Marquise de Guercheville's financial backing, the ship *Jonas* sailed from Honfleur, France, to Port Royal, Nova Scotia, with a contingent of fifty passengers. The *Jonas* was loaded with an abundance of stores, including goats and even horses. Her passengers included the Jesuits Father Quentin and lay brother Gilbert du Thet. Arriving in Port Royal two months later and picking up more Jesuits, Father Pierre Biard and Father Enemond Masse, the *Jonas* set sail again five days later. The *Jonas* and the Jesuits were headed for Norumbega, perhaps still hoping to find the golden city, but fate and fog had other plans. In Father Biard's own words, as quoted in Thwaites's *Jesuit Relations*:

> *Unfavorable winds kept us about five days at Port Royal, and then a propitious Northeaster arising, we departed, intending to go to the river Pentegoet* [the Penobscot], *to the place called Kadesquit* [Bangor], *the site destined for the new colony, and having many great advantages for such a purpose. But God ordained otherwise...the weather changed, and there came upon the sea such a dense fog that we could see no more by day than by night. We had serious misgivings in this time of danger, because in this place there are breakers and rocks, against which we were afraid of striking in the darkness; the wind not permitting us to draw away and stand out to sea.*

There were no lighthouses, foghorns or marker buoys along the coast of Maine in 1613, nor was the vessel *Jonas* equipped with radar or GPS. According to Biard, the ship wrestled in stormy, foggy seas for two days, "veering now to one side, now to another." One can certainly imagine what a frightening state of affairs these Jesuits and their companions were battling. It would seem that only a miracle could bring them safely to shore, any shore. Father Biard continued:

> *In his goodness he hearkened to us, for when evening came on we began to see the stars, and by morning the fogs had all but disappeared. We recognized that we were opposite Mount desert, an island, which the savages call Pemetiq. The pilot turned to the Eastern shore of the Island, and there located us in a large and beautiful port, where we made our thanksgiving to God, raising a Cross and singing to God his praises with the sacrifice of the holy Mass. We called this place and port Saint Sauveur.*

Where the recalcitrant Down East wind had likely blown the Jesuits was right into Frenchman's Bay, beside the Porcupine Islands at Bar Harbor. The first few months were idyllic, as if spent in Eden. Of Mount Desert Island, Baird reported, "This place is a beautiful hill, rising gently from the sea, its sides bathed by two springs," and he further added, "The Harbor especially is as safe as a pond. For, besides being strengthened by the great Island of Mount desert, it is still more protected by certain small Islands which break the currents and the winds."

It wasn't the "currents and the winds" that the Jesuits should have been frightened of. Louis XIII declared the Marquise de Guercheville the sole proprietor of New France in 1613, following the assassination of Henry IV. The French had settlements in Canada and Maine. The Spanish had settlements in more southerly areas, but they never came to Maine. King James I of England founded the Virginia Company of Plymouth in 1606 with hopes of creating English colonies along the coast. There had been an English colony in Maine, which was considered part of Northern Virginia, eventually becoming New England. This was certainly quite confusing, to be sure.

It is no wonder that disaster befell the Jesuits at Saint Sauveur when Englishman Samuel Argall, of the Virginia colony at Jamestown, sailed his sloop of war *Treasurer* into Frenchman's Bay. The *Treasurer* had a large crew and fourteen guns, and Captain Argall had authority from King James to squash violations of his charter of the New World. Argall was serious about protecting the settlement rights of the English, and he is noted for kidnapping Virginia Indian chief Powhatan's famous daughter Pocahontas to ensure the safety of colonists in Jamestown. However, it was at first fog and fishing that brought the *Treasurer* into Frenchman Bay, as Samuel Argall had no knowledge of Saint Sauveur. It was the native Wabanaki who informed Argall of the French after his ship was blown off course in bad weather and fog while he was fishing for cod to bring back down to the Jamestown Colony.

"The English ship came on swifter than an arrow," Father Biard related, "driven by a propitious wind, all screened in pavesade of red, the banners of England flying, and three trumpets and two drums making a horrible din."

The *Jonas* was sitting peacefully at anchor with her sails spread over the deck, being used as awnings to shade the few sailors and master who remained aboard. The French were taken completely by surprise.

"They had fourteen pieces of artillery and sixty musketeers," Father Biard noted. "The first volley from the English was terrible, the whole ship being enveloped in fire and smoke."

After the English fired, the French captain ordered a return fire, but there was nobody on board to obey his order. Brother du Thet, by this time having boarded the *Jonas*, attempted to fire the cannon but didn't think to aim it, so the round was of no use. This demonstration angered the English musketeers, who took aim and fired at Brother du Thet, who fell onto the deck mortally wounded. The rest was child's play for Argall and his men as the musketeers felled a few more Frenchmen before it was finally over. Argall put Father Masse and fourteen others into their longboat, where they crossed the open sea and luckily found a French ship to take them home. The remaining prisoners, including Fathers Biard and Quentin, were taken to Jamestown on the *Treasurer* but were eventually released.

The English broke the Jesuit cross into pieces and, afterward, erected their own in the name of King James. After they tore down the Jesuits' cross and demolished Saint Sauveur, Captain Argall and his men burned the buildings that were left on St. Croix and then raided the French colony at Port Royal.

MOUNT DESERT ISLAND

It would seem, after the expulsion of the Jesuits by Captain Argall in 1613, that the French would have no permanent colony at Ile Des Monts Déserts. In 1688 a self-promoting French entrepreneur, Antoine Laumet, who changed his name to Sieur de La Mothe-Cadillac, obtained a grant from Loius XIV for lands including Mount Desert Island, as well as much of the mainland that today composes most of Hancock County. This grant likely included today's towns of Trenton, Lamoine, Ellsworth, Sullivan and Hancock. Cadillac and his wife only stayed on Mount Desert for a summer, never to return. Perhaps they were afraid of pirates or more English sailors like Argall. Cadillac later went on to found Detroit and left the highest peak on Mount Desert Island with his name.

The native Wabanaki, who knew the island as *Pemetic*, meaning "sloping land," only visited temporarily to hunt and fish, returning to their winter homes at the change of the season. The first people to come to Mount Desert to stay were some Englishmen who came from Gloucester, Massachusetts, in 1761.

There is a timeworn, leather-bound volume that beckoned to me from its place on a bookshelf. The faded, dark cover sported a hand-engraved label, which read *The American Universal Geography*. The book was written by Jedidiah Morse, whom the title page tells the prospective reader is "Minister of the Congregational Church in Charlestown," and it was printed in Boston by Isaiah Thomas and Ebenezer T. Andrews in 1802.

After perusing an index of sorts, I turned to the chapter entitled "District of Maine (Belonging to Massachusetts)." Apparently, Dr. Morse felt it necessary to remind the reader that Maine was not an independent entity. The good doctor did live until he was sixty-five years of age, dying in 1826; he lived to see Maine gain its statehood in 1820. "Mount Desert Island," Morse tells us, "is about 15 miles long and 12 broad, rising in nine lofty summits, often above the clouds." Interestingly, it would seem that the Jesuits made a lasting impression on this region in Maine, as Morse later noted in his chapter on the District of Maine:

> *The remains of the Penobscot tribe are the only Indians who take up their residence in this District. They consist of about 100 families, and live together in regular society at Indian Old Town, which is situated on an island of about 200 acres, in Penobscot River, just above the great falls. They are Roman Catholics, and have a priest, who resides among them and administers the ordinances.*

Morse mentioned nothing about the English settlers from Gloucester. Perhaps that is because his history was first published in 1789 and the number of persons on Mount Desert at that time was considered unremarkable. It is interesting to note that in Morse's history, which is composed of 831 pages, his chapter on the "District of Maine" is only 14 pages long while that entitled "Massachusetts (Proper)" is 49 pages in length.

Not everybody who resided in Massachusetts possessed an indifferent attitude toward the District of Maine. Indeed, Francis Bernard, who was the royal governor of the Province of Massachusetts Bay in 1761, desperately wanted to take possession of Mount Desert Island. After the end of the century and a half of conflict between France and England, which was finally settled in 1760, when the British defeated the French in what was called the Seven Years' War (or French and Indian War in North America), eastern Maine became available for settlement by the English. Governor Bernard managed to persuade King George III to make him sole proprietor of the island in 1764.

Unable to wait until it was made official, in 1761, Bernard managed to convince Abraham Somes and James Richardson of Gloucester to start a settlement on Mount Desert Island, granting them plenty of free land. Bernard knew that Somes had been to the island in 1755, hearing that he had purchased a small island off Mount Desert from an "Indian" for a gallon of rum. A companion of Somes, an Ebenezer Sutton, was supposed to have made a better deal, purchasing the island that bears his name for only two quarts. At any rate, Somes and Richardson settled what is now called "Somesville" in the summer of 1761 and brought their wives and children to the island the following year.

In September 1762, Royal Governor Francis Bernard felt compelled to go Down East and survey his acquisition. With him he brought a contingent of soldiers and had an array of guns on his sloop *Massachusetts*. How excited he must have been, not realizing that after the coming Revolution the appointments of King George would amount to naught.

Governor Bernard kept a journal of the visit to "his" island, and for the entry dated "Oct. 7" he stated:

> *We went on shore and into Somes's log house, found it neat and convenient, though not quite furnished, and in it a notable woman with four pretty girls, clean and orderly. Near it were many fish drying there.*

The islands around Mount Desert were likely occupied by 1762, as Governor Bernard noted in his journal that "four families were settled upon one of the Cranberry Islands, and two families at the head of the river." According to Street in his 1905 history of Mount Desert, Christopher Bartlett was on Bartlett's Island, and John Robertson, Isaac Bunker and Samuel Stanley were staying on Great Cranberry Island during the summer of 1762. Benjamin Spurling, who came from Portsmouth, New Hampshire, was likely the first permanent settler on Great Cranberry and Samuel Hadlock, from Gloucester, the first on Little Cranberry. Aside from being among the first settlers on Little Cranberry, Samuel Hadlock was also the first to commit murder on Mount Desert Island, in 1789.

In his *Last Words and Dying Speech*, Samuel Hadlock described his arrival on the island:

> *I took a small schooner and put on board some stores, and as much of my household goods as I could carry—took my two sons and two daughters with me, and sailed along the Eastern Coast, until we arrived at Mount Desert: where I had never been before. I found a small harbour, lived on board my vessel, and worked on shore, until I built me a log house. In*

> *about three weeks I went back to Chebacco* [Chebacco refers to a part of Massachusetts that is today part of the town of Essex, near Gloucester], *and brought my wife, and the remainder of my goods.*

In 1768, Thomas Richardson and Daniel Gott, my ancestors, also arrived from Gloucester, Massachusetts, to settle on Mount Desert Island. In 1789, Daniel Gott obtained a deed to two islands off Bass Harbor Head and lived on the larger one until his death in 1816. That island became known as Gott's Island. The Richardsons, according to Street, were "of sturdy Scotch-Irish descent." An interesting and little-known fact about the Richardson brothers is that their father, who worked for a Scottish laird, secretly married his employer's daughter, Lady Jane Montgomery, and ran off to America in 1738 to avoid scandal.

Another wave of settlers came from Gloucester, and these included Stephen Richardson and Stephen Gott, along with Andrew Tarr, Benjamin Stanwood and others. Some families from Cape Cod came next; these included Levi Higgins in 1770, Israel Higgins the following year and Ezra Young and others. Indeed, this was the first and only time that expansion shifted to the east instead of westward. The French had lost the recent war, as well as their claim to eastern Maine.

Ah, over the centuries so many have laid claim to this island! After the American Revolution, Francis Bernard's son, John Bernard, was granted much of his father's land. Since John had sided with the Americans during their struggle for independence, the General Court of Massachusetts honored his request in 1785. It would seem that there was another claimant to the island, however, in 1786. The granddaughter of Sieur de Cadillac, a Madame de Grégoire, came out of nowhere and insisted she be awarded her grandfather's lands. Because the new country did not want to offend France, Madame de Grégoire's request was granted, and she was awarded half the island of Mount Desert, as well as some lands on the mainland to the east.

On July 4, 1787, the General Court of Massachusetts appointed Nathan Jones and Thomas Richardson to set the boundary between the Grégoire claim and that of John Bernard and the first settlers. Eventually, Grégoire and Bernard sold off most of their acquisitions.

Early visitors to Mount Desert Island describe the inhabitants as having enough cultivated land to supply themselves with ample produce—usually rye, wheat, barley, potatoes, corn and vegetables. In addition, each family had a boat with which to catch cod, curing and selling or exchanging it for needed goods. Many residents cut cordwood, barrel shooks, staves, shingles and clapboards. There were early mills, and the lumber trade was lucrative. Frenchman's Bay was often filled with vessels whose cargoes included some form of lumber or timber from the island. Cows, poultry and pigs were reported to be in abundance, but there weren't many horses in the early days due to the lack of proper roads.

Reports of piles of lobsters two and three feet high washing up on shore were frequent in the earliest days, as were occasional reports of lobsters reaching four feet in length. Although lobsters were not considered anything special to the first settlers, Wasson described them in his 1878 survey: "The demand for their luxurious flesh is immense; this makes a very great business for our county people. Packing and canning establishments are in successful operation at Castine, Deer Isle, Brooklin, Gouldsboro, Mt. Desert and Cranberry Isles."

The limited amount of forage for livestock was a problem on the island, causing settlers to fight amongst people on the mainland and sometimes with one another over rights to hayfields and woodlots. In 1768, some early settlers, including Abraham Somes, Andrew Tarr, Benjamin Standwood, Daniel Gott and Thomas Richardson, sent a petition to Governor Bernard practically begging him to protect them from others coming on the island and stealing their hay and timber. Below is an excerpt from this petition, as preserved in the Bernard Papers and reprinted in Street's 1905 history:

> *We the inhabitants of mount desart Humbly Craves Your Exelencys Protection against the InCrosins of the Naboring inhabents made upon us Consarning hay for we cannot git hay on ye island to Keep our Stoks as the People Cut the hay before it gits its Groth So that they spoil the marsh… Last summer the People came from the Townshep of No. Six and Cut Part of the North East marsh where we have had a rode this five yeare before we knew thereof & carred off some hay after we Raked & Stacked it, also other hay which we Cut and Staked was Stole.*

This stealing of hay and forage was quite a serious matter and threatened the health of the livestock, which in turn also threatened the livelihood of the settlers. Not only was the hay "Stole," but also it was often taken after it was painstakingly cut, raked and stacked, a process that requires several days' work. It would seem the thieves, in many cases, waited until the hay was ready for harvest and then took it. It is no wonder the colonists were angry. To add insult to injury, people were also coming and removing whatever lumber they wished to take for their own needs. What a tough bunch those first folks must have been to endure the hardships imposed on them by severe weather, unrelenting cold, starvation, sickness and even other settlers.

The residents of the island built schools and churches, as did many of the inhabitants in other New England towns, but it was their proximity to the sea and markedly independent nature that made the people living on Mount Desert Island unique. The breathtaking, rugged beauty of the towering mountains rising out of the Atlantic and scenic rock-strewn shores only added to the island's allure.

Mount Desert was incorporated as the sixty-eighth township in the Province of Maine in February 1779. In April 1795, a vote was passed to divide the "town" of Mount Desert, and the selectmen were instructed to choose its boundary. By February 1796, the Massachusetts legislature had made the division official; the island would be divided into two towns, and the town of Eden was incorporated.

Today, there are four towns on this largest island off the coast of Maine, and they are Mount Desert, Bar Harbor (formerly Eden), Southwest Harbor and Tremont. The origin of the name Bar Harbor is quite simple. At low

The schooner *Mary B. Wellington* off Mount Desert Island. *From the Foss Collection, courtesy of the Penobscot Marine Museum.*

tide, there is a "bar" exposed between Mount Desert Island and nearby Bar Island or Rodick's Island.

The first murder occurred on Mount Desert Island in October 1789. Samuel Hadlock, forty-four, crushed the skull of Eliab Littlefield Gott, twenty-two, after an argument. Hadlock first tried to drown Gott by pushing his head under water three times. When that didn't produce the desired effect, he chased him with a club to a neighbor's house, knocked him down and fractured his skull using a slat from the fence that was in front of the residence. This seems to be the generally accepted version of the story.

It is very interesting that this murder isn't mentioned in any of the classic histories of the island. Luckily, in 1998, some folks from the Mount Desert Island Historical Society, including Alice Long, published a paper entitled "Hadlock Executed This Day," which gives a detailed account of the events that occurred before and after this egregious crime was committed.

Samuel Hadlock came to the island from Gloucester, Massachusetts, to engage in lumbering. He wanted to make use of the large tracts of virgin timber along what became Hadlock Pond, in an area that is now known as Northeast Harbor, and operated mills that were powered by water. One morning in October, Hadlock was busy working in his sawmill and became desirous of spirits. By his own admission in his *Last Words and Dying Speech*, as reprinted by the Mount Desert Historical Society, he

> *rose early in the morning, went out to work as usual for about two or three hours, and then went into the house. Being very thirsty I made some drink with water, rum and molasses, and drank once or twice. I felt dizzy in my head, and a good deal disordered in my mind.*

After drinking, Hadlock walked through his field until he came to the house of John Manchester, a neighbor. An argument ensued between Hadlock and Manchester's wife, which resulted in Hadlock dragging the woman outside by the hair. At this point, James Richardson Jr. happened by and defused the situation, convincing Hadlock to leave. "I then stamped on the floor and said never was a man so ill used," Hadlock stated, and then he "went directly home."

Unfortunately, Mr. Hadlock didn't stay at home and ended up walking through his field once more. This time, he called to Eliab Gott and Daniel Tarr, who were crossing a nearby river in a canoe. Witnesses said Hadlock pulled Gott from his boat and held him under water and then drove both Gott and Tarr back to the Manchester home, chasing them with a club. James Richardson was still there, at the insistence of Mrs. Manchester, and Hadlock threatened him as well. Samuel Hadlock's story was a bit different. He stated:

> *James Richardson came out of the house, seized me by the throat, shoved me against a fence, and kept smiting me in the face. Then Gott seized me by the hair and by the nose, while Richardson bent my neck over the fence and almost strangled me.*

Soon afterward, an enraged Samuel Hadlock killed Eliab Gott by crushing his skull and was eventually "remanded to gaol and put in irons." Hadlock stood trial and was convicted of murder and sentenced to be "hanged by the neck until dead." Understandably, Samuel Hadlock did not wish to hang, so he cleverly escaped from jail by digging a hole beneath the hearth and "about midnight went through the hole I had made and crept along under the goal, dug under the sill unbeknown to any person and made my escape."

Making his way along the coast, Hadlock found work on fishing schooners and went by the name of Gilbert. Eventually, he was discovered on a fishing schooner owned by his son-in-law, who had sworn that he was not on board. When a member of the search party, Jacob Reed, went below deck to warm up, he heard the snap of a trigger. Hadlock had attempted to shoot the men in the boarding party, but the gun didn't fire. Hadlock then began to stab Reed several times with his bayonet, until he was apprehended. Next, in Samuel Hadlock's own words:

> *I was taken by nineteen armed men, who robbed me of six dollars and a half in cash, one silk handkerchief, a pair of stockings, sundry fishing geers, and my gun and bayonet. I was then carried to Portland gaol, where I was confined about a week. Then brought back to Pownalborough, where I have remained in irons until this fated hour.*

Hadlock was hanged on October 28, 1790, exactly one year after Eliab Gott died. Interestingly, Samuel Hadlock fell through the noose the first time the platform was knocked from under him. Witnesses said that he showed no fear, and the second time he was "launched into eternity." Mr. Hadlock left some advice for us:

> *I do now solemnly caution and warn all persons to avoid quarrels and contentions with any one; especially with such as would irritate and raise your passions; whereby you may rashly do that which may afterwards cause you bitter repentance.*

Samuel Hadlock was executed at the Pownalborough Courthouse, located in present-day Dresden, Maine, on the banks of the Kennebec River. The courthouse, which was built in 1761, has known such famous visitors as Robert Treat Paine, John Adams and Benedict Arnold. It is the only pre–Revolutionary War courthouse still in existence in the state of Maine.

There have been so many references to Frenchman's Bay that by now the reader must be curious as to the origin of the name. According to James Sullivan in his 1795 *History of the District of Maine*, Frcnchman's Bay was so named due to one particular incident. According to Sullivan, when Sieur De Monts left the French encampment of St. Croix back in the spring of 1604 and headed south to Maine, he had in his company a French cleric whose name was Nicholas D'Aubri. It would seem that Nicholas became quite curious about the Down East coast, eventually insisting he be set ashore. According to William Williamson in his later 1839 history of Maine, D'Aubri likely went ashore "between the Union and Narraguagus rivers," which could possibly have been near present-day Hancock, and became lost. The sailor who had taken him to shore could wait no longer and returned to his ship. According to Sullivan's 1795 history regarding D'Aubri:

> *His account of his sufferings was no doubt very pitiful; for he remained three weeks in the wilderness, wandering from place to place under the most terrible apprehensions, until the boat of the same vessel, by accident found him on shore, and restored him to the ship's company. From this accident the waters of the whole bay of Fundy were called Frenchman's Bay.*

According to Samuel Eliot Morison in his 1960 *Story of Mount Desert Island*, Frenchman's Bay was so named because during the French and Indian War French warships anchored in the harbor. I have also found, from many sources, the explanation that the bay was named after Champlain, its early French discoverer.

After Champlain's visit to the island, explorer Henry Hudson appeared, but for a different reason. Perhaps the very first attempt by a European to do any shipbuilding or repair on Mount Desert Island was on the *Half Moon* by Henry Hudson and his crew in 1609. In order to replace a foremast that had been lost in a storm, Hudson went ashore to cut a tree. According to the journal written by Hudson's first mate and log keeper Robert Juet on June 15, "We had a great storme, and spent ouer-boord our fore-mast." On July 18, 1609, with the *Half Moon* anchored in what is now Somes Sound, "we went on shoare and cut us a fore Mast, then at noone we came aboord againe."

It took Hudson's crew five days to finish the replacement mast, and all the time the *Half Moon* lay at Mount Desert the men caught many "great coddes" and lobsters. By July 23, according to Juet, "at eleven of the clocke, our fore Mast was finished, and we brought it aboord, and set it into the step, and in the after-noone we rigged it."

The native Wabanaki, who were used to trading with the French, had been friendly to Hudson and his men during the time they were on the island. Unfortunately, before Hudson left Mount Desert on July 25, Juet related, "we manned our boat and scute with twelve men and Muskets, and two stone Pieces or Murderers, and drave the Savages from their Houses." Hudson's men also took the natives' furs and goods before leaving the island.

Although Hudson's crew fashioned a mast for the *Half Moon*, they certainly didn't build any ships, though there were ample raw materials readily available. It was the accessibility of large tracts of timber and proximity to the ocean that made the island a prime location for the construction of ships.

Naturally, shipbuilding on Mount Desert Island became an important industry, and according to information compiled by historian Ralph Stanley, there were 368 vessels built on Mount Desert Island between 1782 and 1902. These vessels were mostly schooners; some brigs, sloops and brigantines; and a few barks. "Shipbuilding began on Mount Desert Island soon after the settlers came in the early 1760s," according to local historian and shipbuilder Ralph Stanley.

> *I think the settlers came not with the intentions to build ships but rather to build a home for themselves. They found a lot of timber growing on the island and there were streams and tidal coves where a mill could be set up harnessing the waterpower to saw logs into lumber, which was sold and shipped away in vessels.*

A long way from Frenchman's Bay, the schooner *Theoline* waits at Pier 11 on the East River in Manhattan, 1933. *Photo by Percy Loomis Sperr. From the Foss Collection, courtesy of the Penobscot Marine Museum.*

What better authority on shipbuilding than a man who has himself built seventy ships and whose ancestors were among many of the first to settle on Mount Desert? Mr. Stanley's family never left the island and has been there since 1762. The island and the seas that crash on its shores, as well as the vessels and the men who have pushed them over the centuries, have left some remnant, a trace in the blood.

"When I was a small boy, I would get someone to walk up the road with me," Mr. Stanley explained, "to where I could look out across the cove and see the schooner anchored there."

Ralph Stanley is speaking of the four-masted schooner *Theoline*, which was built in Rockland, Maine, in 1917 and was a frequent visitor to Mount Desert Island. The *Theoline* is one of many wooden-hulled, four-masted schooners that were built during the First World War to take advantage of the high freights paid for cargoes during wartime. Ralph Stanley also recalled:

> *It has been said that when Captain John Latty brought coal to the Underwood factory at Bass Harbor* [at this Mount Desert factory they canned lobster, clams and sardines] *in the* Theoline, *that while approaching the harbor with a southwest wind, he would reduce sail,*

> *and while still making headway drop his anchor. When the anchor fetched up he would pay out chain and as the vessel swung around she would lay right abreast the head of the dock. Captain Latty also brought cans to the factory from Lubec, where the cans were manufactured.*

The *Theoline* was also seen tied up to a wharf in New York City, where she made frequent visits. That city became her home port in 1943, but soon afterward she would become a casualty of war.

"I believe the *Theoline* was chartered to carry munitions to Africa and was torpedoed and sunk during World War II," Mr. Stanley explained.

Of the many, many stories of shipwrecks and tragedy regarding vessels and crews with ties to the island, Mr. Stanley had only to say, "The sea gives a lot, but it also takes a lot."

Visitors to Mount Desert, according to *Harper's New Monthly Magazine* published in August 1872, noticed this about the people of the island:

> *Their life is altogether peculiar. The women do most of what there is in the way of farming, while the men, from early boyhood, are upon or in the water, chiefly as fishermen, but always as sailors, and unquestionably the best sailors in the world.*

These visitors to the island in 1872 were representative of a special type of tourist. The "summer people" came to Mount Desert and other parts of coastal Maine seasonally and first called themselves "rusticators."

Much has been written about the rusticators who started coming to the island in the mid-nineteenth century. Like the early visitors to Mount Desert and Down East Maine, the rusticators were also looking for a Norumbega. They were looking for the romantic, fabled lands of breathtaking beauty and rugged oceanfront scenes that were depicted in the popular artwork of the day. The painters of the Hudson River School, the most famous of whom included Fredrick Church, Hermann Herzog and Thomas Cole, portrayed many scenes from Mount Desert Island and coastal Maine in their artwork. These painters were strongly influenced by romanticism, a popular school of thought that evolved partly in response to rising population growth and industrialization, serving as a means of escape through a heightened interest in experiencing nature.

By 1850, Thomas Cole and Fredrick Church had traveled to Mount Desert Island, particularly Bar Harbor, and painted many local scenes. These works

The steamship *Norumbega* en route between Bar Harbor and the Mount Desert Ferry in Hancock. *Courtesy of the Hancock Historical Society.*

of art became unintended advertisements for the area that inspired them, and soon folks began to visit the island looking for their own inspiration.

The first visitors roomed with the residents of the island, providing them with a lucrative alternative form of income. Although not particularly suited to operate boardinghouses, the island's inhabitants quickly found that they could make a business of it during the clement summer months. The first hotel on Bar Harbor was built by Tobias Roberts in 1867, and soon many others followed. These early summer people, or rusticators, came to the coast of Maine to experience "rustic" surroundings and originally intended to "rough it," not bringing the comforts of home with them. This soon changed, however, as many lavish hotels sprung up later in the century.

In 1870, the only way to reach Bar Harbor was to travel by stage from Bangor or by steamship from Portland, which only ran twice a week. These means of travel to the island were uncomfortable and time-consuming. In 1884, when the Maine Central Railroad built the Mount Desert Ferry in the town of Hancock and began running its steamships directly to Bar Harbor, tourists swarmed to the island en masse. Mount Desert Island would never be the same, and neither would Hancock.

HANCOCK POINT, THE MOUNT DESERT FERRY AND THE BAR HARBOR EXPRESS

The Mount Desert Ferry in Hancock was once the gateway to Bar Harbor. What is it that keeps one place so familiar while the other is so nearly lost to the passing of time? Whatever it is, Hancock has been curiously silent for decades. It is time, however, for the town of Hancock to give up its secrets once again.

When I first saw Hancock Point, I was standing on the deck of the last working four-masted schooner, the *Margaret Todd* out of Bar Harbor. Although she was built in 1998 and is steel-hulled, the *Margaret Todd* carries 4,800 square feet of sail and well represents her predecessors that plied the seas more than a century ago. The topmasts, gaffs and booms are all made of Maine spruce, and most of the woodwork on the vessel was completed right on Mount Desert Island.

As his vessel lay in Bar Harbor, Steven Pagels, captain of the *Margaret Todd*, surveyed the thick shroud of fog and mist that had descended on the Porcupine Islands, nearly obliterating them from view, rising and falling as if to tease the diligent observer.

"The wind comes off the mountains on this island later in the day and blows the fog away from this harbor, off the Porcupines," Captain Pagels announced, gesturing. "This fog should soon disappear."

I watched as the fog that had completely enveloped the Porcupine Islands slowly receded and then returned. I heard a foghorn somewhere in the

Where the past meets the present, a modern cruise ship shares Frenchman's Bay with the four-masted *Margaret Todd* at her home port of Bar Harbor. *Photo by author.*

distance, then quiet and then water lapping against the hull of the schooner. Soon we were underway, and the sun began to peek out from above the murkiness. It was getting brighter aloft.

The spanker boom slowly creaked and shifted as a breeze came up in Frenchman's Bay, and Hancock Point came into view over the port bow. From my vantage point on the schooner's deck, the imposing, rock-strewn shoreline gave the observer no indication that it was part of the mainland rather than Mount Desert Island itself. It was easy to see why the summer folks built their cottages on Hancock Point. They wanted to have their own commanding views of Cadillac Mountain rising majestically up into the clouds on Mount Desert Island.

Much has been written about Mount Desert Island and much, much more about Bar Harbor. The unassuming town of Hancock, though—or its once-celebrated Hancock Point—is for the most part unknown. The two places are but a short distance apart, separated only by a short expanse of salt water: Frenchman's Bay. Although Hancock Point is actually part of the town of Hancock and not a separate entity, it seems to have developed its own distinctive personality, especially in regard to its noteworthy summer colony.

The early history of settlement in the area begins in the latter part of the eighteenth century with an interesting Revolutionary War shipmaster, Captain Agreen Crabtree. Crabtree was master of the privateer schooner *Hannah and Molley*, taking many prizes during the war. Captain Crabtree plundered a dozen vessels with British ties between 1776 and 1778, during a time when acts of piracy such as this were considered commendable and often quite profitable. According to *A History of the Town of Hancock*, published in 1978, we know that Agreen Crabtree and his sons

> *built their houses, laid out their gardens—chiefly potatoes, beans and squashes—planted apple trees and raspberries and felled the heavily forested acres of spruce, maple and birch and engaged in timber trading.*

Crabtree's Neck was part of the town of Sullivan; the town of Hancock was not to be incorporated until 1828. Although Captain Crabtree was first to settle Crabtree's Neck, there were other families who came there as well. However, few enjoyed this expanse of mostly undisturbed acreage until after the Civil War, when the nearby town of Ellsworth needed a Baptist minister.

In the summer of 1867, after being urged by members of his congregation to visit Crabtree's Point to see the beautiful view of Frenchman's Bay and Mount Desert Island, Dr. Francis Hazelwood finally conceded. Afterward, he was never the same. He became immediately enamored of the place and was determined to purchase property of his own, building the first summer cottage on the point in 1876. Not surprisingly, young Dr. Hazelwood, being from Boston, had lots of well-educated and distinguished acquaintances that he would eventually invite to his summer place. These friends naturally became similarly afflicted by the charm of the point, buying their own property and building their own summer cottages.

One does not usually associate Victorian New England with epicurean pursuits; at least, one does not expect them to be spoken of. I was surprised to find the following advice offered by Wasson in his 1878 *Survey of Hancock County*: "To the seekers of pleasure, or to those who would spend a season imbibing the exhilarating air of our ocean, we know of no more inviting locality than Crabtree's Neck."

Early aerial view of Hancock Point. *Courtesy of the Hancock Historical Society.*

It was this rugged beauty and pastoral, untouched elegance, including impressive views of Mount Desert Island, that brought throngs of "summer folk" to Hancock Point. This interesting summer colony consisted of intellectuals, including college professors, scientists and writers. Their presence made an impact on the community and gave rural Hancock a bit of a cosmopolitan air.

Soon, civilization would descend on the little town of Hancock en masse, all because of the rising popularity of Hancock Point and its proximity to Mount Desert Island and Bar Harbor. In 1872, there was a steamer service to Rockland from nearby Sullivan, and in 1876, a wharf was built on Hancock Point for the steamships. By 1882, Hancock Point had its own post office; in 1886, a shore road was constructed; and in 1888, a lighthouse was erected. Next, a hotel appeared, called the Tarrantine, named after the native tribe that once frequented the area. There was even, unbelievably, a golf course. The rest of Hancock at this time remained primarily a rural farming and fishing community, and the contrast between one part of town and the rest was significant.

Hancock was bustling. In 1884, at nearby McNeil Point in Hancock, the Mount Desert Ferry began operations. The unpretentious little town of Hancock had become the gateway to Bar Harbor. The Maine Central Railroad owned the locomotives and the steamers, and it also built the wharves and the elegant station house. It was not unusual, during peak season, to have trains arriving and departing several times a day. There was a turntable or roundtable where the giant locomotives could literally be turned around for their return journey back to the big cities. Entrepreneurs from the nearby city of Bangor built a first-class one-hundred-room hotel and resort called The Bluffs overlooking picturesque Frenchman's Bay.

The first train was known as the Mount Desert Limited; it later became the Bar Harbor Express in 1902. These trains were equipped with luxurious accommodations and state-of-the-art technology, including carved gilded woodwork and color-coordinated curtains, seats and cloth, not to mention electric buttons at each window in case one wished to call the porter.

There were also many private railway cars that frequented the Mount Desert Ferry, owned by such influential people as the Vanderbilts, Rockefellers, Searses, Morgans and Pulitzers, to name a few. In 1899, President Benjamin Harrison arrived and was greeted by a cheering crowd. In 1910, President William Howard Taft also visited the rail terminal on his way to Bangor.

Some of the steamers that traveled from the Mount Desert Ferry to Bar Harbor were the *Sebenoe*, *Sappho*, *Sieur de Monts*, *Samoset*, *Moosehead*, *Rangely* and *Norumbega*. These steamers varied in size. The *Sebenoe*, named after the famous Kennebec chief, was 91 feet long and 18 feet wide. The *Sappho*, named for the Grecian poet, was 156 feet in length and 26 feet wide, and the *Norumbega* was 146 feet long and 26 feet wide.

The steamer *Norumbega* ready to take passengers from the Mount Desert Ferry to Bar Harbor. *Courtesy of the Hancock Historical Society.*

A sort of travel guide published in 1886 entitled *Bar Harbor and Mount Desert Island* informed the reader:

> *Passengers can leave Boston in elegant palace cars at nine o'clock in the morning and before eight the same evening they can be at their hotel or cottage at Bar Harbor. Or they can leave Boston at seven o'clock in the evening by sleeping cars, arrive in Bangor at five-thirty the following morning and at Bar Harbor at eight-thirty.*

It is interesting to note that the same publication also states:

> *Since the opening of the Mount Desert Branch of the Maine Central Railroad, a new impulse has been given to the travel in this direction, and the number of visitors to Bar Harbor has more than quadrupled within the last two years.*

The unpretentious little town of Hancock certainly became the gateway to one of the most prestigious coastal resorts in the Northeast, and it seemed to happen almost overnight. It is no wonder that on August 4, 1899, a tragic accident occurred. There was an unusual attraction in Frenchman's Bay on that day—the warships of the North Atlantic Squadron were on display. The Spanish-American War was over, and guests were encouraged to visit these battleships. The sailors and officers were dressed in their finest uniforms, and there would even be a fancy dress ball at Bar Harbor. Not surprisingly, there were record numbers of people descending on the Mount Desert Ferry Terminal. Somehow, as is often the case, word got to the passengers who were still on the train that the steamer *Sappho* could not accommodate everyone and consequently would have to make several runs. Naturally, everybody wanted to make the first trip on the steamer rather than spend hours of their holiday waiting at the wharf. The calamity that ensued was disastrous.

The gangplank from the wharf to the ferryboats was wooden, forty feet long and only ten feet wide, and it was moveable in order to accommodate the rising and falling of the tides at various times during the day. This gangplank was never intended to support hundreds of people, but on August 4, 1899, there were over two hundred souls heaped on it, likely pushing and shoving to maintain their places in line for the steamer. When the structure collapsed, more than two hundred frightened people plunged into the icy seawater, while over one hundred bystanders watched helplessly in horror. The *New York Times* reported that "a struggling, screaming mass of humanity was plunged into the water fifteen feet below the wharf."

The terrified victims were trapped between the wharf pilings and the steamship, and with no room for escape, many were pushed deeper into the water by those who struggled for their lives above them. The *New York Times* article continued:

> *Ropes and life preservers were thrown to the crowd, but in the panic the people in the water clutched one another, and many sank thus in groups in a death grapple. Many persons taken from the water were unconscious, and were revived with difficulty.*
>
> *The dreadful nature of the accident was not comprehended for at least a minute by those who were the last to leave the train, although the scene changed instantly from one of holiday gaiety to a death struggle.*

The steamer *Cymbria* came from Bar Harbor with four physicians as soon as word of the calamity reached the island, and a train was quickly sent from Bangor with more doctors and nurses. Many of the injured were taken to the Bluffs Hotel to be treated. The freight house at the wharf was made into a makeshift morgue, and the bodies were taken there for identification. Twenty-one persons drowned, and one of the men who lost his life in the disaster had been on his way to Bar Harbor to see his fiancée.

The waters of Frenchman's Bay have certainly witnessed many tragic events, some of which history may never again recall. We only know of the death of the man who was to meet his fiancée because I found a yellowed newspaper clipping in an old file cabinet. What else have these waters been keeping secret? It would seem that many interesting visitors have appeared between the shores of Mount Desert Island and Hancock Point.

On August 4, 1914, an unlikely caller quietly crept into a fog-shrouded Frenchman's Bay at just about daybreak. When the morning mists lifted, people awoke to find an enormous ocean liner anchored near the Porcupine Islands and Mount Desert. At first it appeared to be the British White Star Line *Olympic*, sister ship to the recently lost *Titanic*, with her four distinctive black smokestacks. However, the *Olympic* was supposed to have been headed for New York, and everybody knew that. People who were curious actually wired New York inquiring about the *Olympic* and asked why she was lying near Bar Harbor.

The vessel that was mistaken for the *Olympic* was actually the German *Kronprinzessin Cecilie*, one of the largest luxury liners in the world. The *Kronprinzessin Cecilie* was launched in December 1906, was 707 feet in length and 72 feet wide and could carry 1,970 passengers. She was one of only four elegant liners and the largest, referred to as "Kaiser class" vessels. She had been en route to Plymouth, England, when war broke out between the two countries. The War to End All Wars had started; it was the beginning of World War I. It was certainly bad timing for the *Cecilie*, for she was carrying nearly 1,600 people, $10.6 million in gold bullion and $3.0 million in silver bars!

Since war had just broken out between Britain and Germany, the *Kronprinzessin Cecilie*, known to be headed for England, would certainly have been intercepted and robbed of her vast treasure. Charles Polack, captain of the *Cecilie*, decided to change course and head for the United States, which was then a neutral country. Polack was, not surprisingly, alarmed that he happened to have such valuable cargo on board when war was declared. One of his wealthy passengers, who had frequently summered on Bar Harbor and knew the bay well, suggested the vessel anchor at that port.

Hoping to cross the Atlantic undiscovered, Polack hoped he could trick observers into believing the *Kronprinzessin Cecilie* was in fact the British White Star Line *Olympic*, which was twelve hours ahead on a course to New York. He cleverly found volunteers to cover the *Cecilie*'s silver smokestacks with black bands so she would appear to be the *Olympic* and crossed the Atlantic that night with the lights on deck extinguished and the portholes covered, not even using the foghorn. Luckily, the giant liner didn't collide with another vessel in the fog and darkness.

Due to the immense vessel's great draft, it was impossible to bring her close enough to any landing, so she simply lay in the bay with her many passengers and millions in bullion. Many of the *Cecilie*'s passengers were infuriated that they had been diverted to the United States. The revenue cutter *Androscoggin* was ordered to Bar Harbor to stand by the *Cecilie* to guard her treasure. The steamship *Norumbega* took the passengers off ship, a feat that took several days. The gold and silver were another matter. The forty tons of treasure were transported across Frenchman's Bay to the railroad terminal in Hancock by the revenue cutter *Androscoggin*.

There were forty armed guards, as well as the contingent of marines, as the $10.6 million in gold and $3.0 million in silver bars were loaded into four

The *Kronprinzessin Cecilie* at a German port.

steel express cars and sent off to New York. Interestingly, after the treasure left Hancock, it is unclear even today where exactly it went.

The *Kronprinzessin Cecilie* was eventually seized by the United States and renamed *Mount Vernon*; guns were added, and the vessel was repainted in the camouflage pattern typical of the day (dazzle) and employed in the war effort as a troop ship.

There were more than summer folks and luxury liners that came to Hancock Point. On the evening of January 1, 1945, FBI director J. Edgar Hoover held a press conference, during which time he detailed the activities of two Nazi spies who had been recently arrested in New York City. Hoover announced that the two men—William Curtis Colepaugh, twenty-six, a U.S. citizen, and Erich Gimpel, thirty-five, a native of Germany—had been trained in both espionage and sabotage. The FBI director went on to explain that a German U-boat had lain off the coast of Maine for a week, in Frenchman's Bay, between the fashionable resort of Bar Harbor and Hancock Point, which Hoover described as "a remote Maine fishing village."

The submarine was *U-1230*, and she was commanded by twenty-seven-year-old Hans Hilbig. While she lay on the ocean bottom near Mount Desert Rock, the crew listened to fishing boats that were working just above them, one anchoring almost directly overhead. On November 29, 1944, after dark and still completely submerged, *U-1230* headed into Frenchman's Bay. Just off Crabtree Point, the vessel rose to the surface, and preparations were made to land the saboteurs. The two men came ashore in a rubber boat rowed by crew members. They carried loaded revolvers, cameras, secret inks, explosives, fraudulent documents (including U.S. Navy discharge papers) and $60,000 in American currency. Luckily for the pair, they were spotted by a taxi driver who lived in Hancock and then driven to the city of Bangor, about thirty-five miles away. From Bangor, they took a train to Boston. Eventually, they arrived in New York City, where they purchased expensive clothing and lived lavishly; during this time, they also bought materials to construct a short-wave radio transmitter to communicate with Germany.

On January 2, 1945, nearly every newspaper in the United States and Canada carried the story about the Nazi spies who had been landed by a German U-boat on the coast of Maine. A particularly detailed account of how the two spies were recognized in Hancock comes from an unlikely source, the *Lawrence Journal-World*, published in faraway Lawrence, Kansas. The article is entitled "Hoover Warns of Espionage Plans, Nazi Saboteurs Caught on East Coast":

> *In the remote Maine fishing village, Deputy Sheriff Dana Hodgkins said his son, Harvard, 17, a high school student, spotted the men the night they landed, walking along a snow covered highway near his home.*
>
> *Hodgkins said his son, a high school senior, was returning home from a dance about midnight, through snow. He became suspicious, the sheriff said, and followed the pair until they disappeared into the woods. The boy told his parents and Sheriff Hodgkins notified the FBI.*
>
> *Hodgkins said Mrs. Mary Forni of Hancock Point also saw the men and their tracks on the night of November 29 and reported the incident.*

Mary Forni, whose husband taught school in nearby Franklin, Maine, was driving to her home in Hancock late that night when she saw two men walking down the road carrying bundles. It was snowing moderately that late November evening, and Mary certainly thought that what she saw was odd, to say the least, so she reported it to Sheriff Hodgkins. The next day, Hodgkins, quite curious by that time, decided to investigate and followed the tracks of the suspicious pair to the waterfront, where he could see signs that a boat had landed. That was enough to convince him to contact the FBI.

In the report of the interrogation of the two German agents issued on January 13, 1945, by the U.S. Navy Department, Gimpel was described as "a professional German espionage agent" and Colepaugh, whose home address was listed as Niantic, Connecticut, as "a somewhat unstable New Englander." The report also described the activities of *U-1230* on the evening of November 29, 1944, and the section regarding the submarine's passage from Frenchman's Bay toward Hancock Point may be of some interest to the reader:

> *The U-boat, once inside the Bay, did not follow the normal channel but proceeded between Porcupine Island and Iron Bound Island. At about 2230, she was about a half-mile offshore. A white house on Crabtree Point was sighted and the U-boat surfaced with her decks awash and only her conning tower above water.*
>
> *The U-boat circled around to within a few hundred yards of the shore. A rubber boat was brought up from below and inflated by a special line which ran through the conning tower hatch and connected with the electric compressor. Colepaugh stated that the inflation was absolutely soundless. Two unarmed members of the ships' company rowed the two agents ashore and then returned to the U-boat.*

Colepaugh and Gimpel were both sentenced to be executed as German spies, but after spending years in prison, they were finally released by President Truman. *U-1230* went on to sink the 5,500-ton Canadian vessel *Cornwallis* before returning to Germany on February 23, 1945.

By now, I suppose that most folks Down East have forgotten what a busy place Hancock Point and the Mount Desert Ferry once were, from their simple beginnings to their heydays. Today's tourists have never known. One would never imagine, driving through the picturesque and seemingly untouched town of Hancock today, that at one time there was a railroad coming straight from New York and Boston that brought summer folks, even presidents and millionaires, into this small Maine coastal town.

Perhaps one could say, regarding the relationship between Hancock and Mount Desert Island, that for the most part, the two histories are inextricably linked. The relationship between Hancock, Hancock Point, the Mount Desert Ferry and the Bar Harbor Express is certainly an interesting one, and one that has been overlooked and left undusted for over half a century.

"Whenever you said you were going to the island," Lois Crabtree Johnson, curator of the Hancock Historical Society, recalled, "you meant you were going to Mount Desert. There are certainly lots of islands around here, but in Hancock, Mount Desert was *the island*, and everybody knew it."

The Hancock Point Lighthouse, also known as Crabtree Ledge Light, was constructed in 1888 because of the increasing traffic in Frenchman's Bay due to all the steamships going back and forth to Mount Desert.

"Nobody cared about the schooners running onto the ledge," Lois recalled, smiling. "But when all the summer people came, they had to put that lighthouse up so the steamers wouldn't get into any trouble out there."

"What happened to it?" I asked, as I had just been to Hancock Point and didn't see any lighthouse.

"It fell over in 1950," Lois replied. "Not too long ago, some divers reported that the remains were lying out there in a pile on the bottom of the bay."

The demise of the lighthouse seemed to signal the end of Hancock's romance with Bar Harbor and the upper echelon of society. Many factors contributed to the decline of the golden era of the Mount Desert Ferry, but the most likely culprit was probably the opening of the causeway to Mount Desert Island in 1931. The world was changing, and it was doing so at an alarming rate. The advent of the automobile ushered in a whole new world as the earlier age fell hopelessly into obscurity.

In 1957, the Maine Central Railroad ended passenger service to Ellsworth, and in 1959 it abandoned the track to the ferry terminal in Hancock.

The summer people still came to Hancock Point, although the Bar Harbor Express was gone. One really didn't seem to have anything to do with the other. The folks who visited "the Point" clearly didn't want to go to Bar Harbor; instead, they preferred a more sequestered location.

The relationship between Maine year-round residents and the "summer people" is an interesting one. Summer people were many cuts above "tourists" because they had an investment in the land and made a commitment to the community. In addition, the summer people provided employment opportunities that were invaluable in many rural communities where local work was not easily found. There might have been some occasional discord, but no more than can be reasonably expected when people with vastly different upbringings, cultures and socioeconomic backgrounds come together in one place.

The summer folks were "very gracious," according to Lois. She remembers waiting tables, serving food and doing dusting for Hancock's seasonal guests back in the summers of 1945 and 1946.

"I did the dining room dishes," Lois explained. "The cook did the kitchen dishes."

Pausing a moment to reflect, she added, "My aunt worked for the post office, and she also delivered meals. On Saturdays, she would bring poultry to the back door." Lois smiled. "But when she delivered the mail, she went to the front door."

Whether they were called seasonal visitors, rusticators or just plain summer folks, their influence on the residents of Maine has been a beneficial one. They shared their vastly different culture and life experiences, making a positive impact on the local community while holding in common their love for the state of Maine.

A BRIEF HISTORY OF THE TOWN OF HANCOCK, MAINE

Rather than by sea, I came into Hancock Village by way of U.S. Coastal Route 1. Coming from Portland, I headed north and passed through lots of prominent coastal communities, including Rockland, Camden, Belfast and Searsport. By the time I reached Ellsworth, I knew that Hancock wasn't too far away. Ellsworth is a fine, historic city with lots of brick buildings and a certain bygone flavor about it. After passing through Ellsworth, the driver has a choice and is informed by signage that he can either remain on the main thoroughfare heading toward "Bar Harbor & Acadia Park" or bear left onto the "Down East Highway," which is actually Coastal Route 1. Luckily, the unpleasant strip malls encountered on this stretch of roadway will come to an abrupt end, as if it is understood that the throngs of tourists no longer pass this way. As the traveler leaves the mad whir of the twenty-first century farther and farther behind, nearing one's destination, a sign with the words "Carrying Place" appears to the right. The next sign reads, "Entering the Village of Hancock."

At the time of the Bar Harbor Express, Hancock Village was the last place the train passed through before reaching the Mount Desert Ferry. According to the 1886 travel booklet *Bar Harbor & Mount Desert Island*:

> *Ellsworth Falls is a thriving village where power is obtained from the Union river and a large lumber business is carried on, and Ellsworth, the*

> *next station, is a beautiful little city situated at the head of navigation on the same river. Hancock Village with its neat white cottages is soon passed, and the next and last station is Mount Desert Ferry, situated on the easterly side of Frenchman's Bay.*

When one enters Hancock today, the village green—or monumental lot, as it is known to townspeople—is a prominent landmark with its statues to war veterans, the most notable being the statue to Civil War soldiers. There is also a small gazebo that suggests to the passerby that it might be a good spot to pause and reflect; the aroma of freshly cut grass paired with the shade offered on a warm summer day enticed me to stop and do that very thing.

Across from the green is the Union Congregational Church, quite conspicuous with its white steeple ascending upward toward the heavens in proper New England style. Next to the village green, the other prominent building is the town hall, also white, built in 1883. As it was an entirely beautiful, idyllic sort of summer day, I decided to walk around and try to find the old railroad tracks that were once part of the Bar Harbor Express service, but I couldn't locate them. So I got back into my vehicle and headed for the historical society, a stone's throw away.

I pulled my Ford truck into the gravel parking lot of Hancock Town Hall, where the Hancock Historical Society is located on the second floor. The gleaming sun shone on the whitest of clouds, their brilliance resonating against the backdrop of a gorgeous blue sky. The air was crisp, with perhaps the slightest hint of an ocean breeze, and it was about seventy-five degrees. It was perfect weather for Down East Maine in August, perfect weather for anywhere on the planet.

I sat on the bench seat of the old truck, basking in the serenity of the moment, drinking in the best of the fresh Maine air when I suddenly spotted Lois Crabtree Johnson, curator of the Hancock Historical Museum.

"I'll be right there," I yelled, not wanting to be late for my appointment. "Just give me a minute to roll up my windows."

"Oh, you don't have to roll up your windows. It doesn't look like rain," Lois remarked, smiling pleasantly.

It was then that I realized how little the town of Hancock, Maine, has changed over the years, and it was at that moment that I saw its true value. Surely, here was a town where time has slowed to nearly a stop. What better place to find history?

The stairway leading to the second floor was winding and steep, but the treasures located upstairs were well worth the moderate amount of exertion that it took to get there. I noticed a familiar musty smell becoming stronger as I ascended the narrow staircase and knew that I was about to enter a realm of artifacts belonging to people and times long passed. The timeworn pine board floor creaked as I passed over it to survey the contents of the large, open room. There were farm implements, horseshoes, Victorian clothing, early photographs, furniture, benches, postcards, letters and booklets. There were rows of file cabinets and shelves full of books and a row of long tables at the center of the room that were covered with yellowed documents and discolored envelopes. Amidst all of this and quite overwhelmed, I asked Lois, "Where should I begin?"

Hancock is situated in Hancock County between the towns of Franklin, Lamoine, Sullivan and Ellsworth, the county seat. According to A.J. Coolidge and J.B. Mansfield, in their *History and Description of New England* published in 1859, Hancock was incorporated in 1828, "the greater part of it having been set off from the town of Sullivan. Tracts were also annexed to it from

The cob-sized painted pony is hooked to a sample of Yankee ingenuity. This slick two-wheeled homemade rig is made from 1930s Ford V8 wheels, a nineteenth-century wagon seat and a handmade box. Perhaps this was an answer to World War II fuel rationing. *Courtesy of the Hancock Historical Society.*

No. 3 Township, and from Trenton." Hancock was named for Patriot John Hancock, first governor of the Commonwealth of Massachusetts and signer of the Declaration of Independence, but before the Europeans came, the area was known as Waukeag to the native people. *Waukeag* simply meant "a seal."

Although the town of Hancock was incorporated in 1828, its history goes back much further than that. The early history of Hancock is not surprisingly similar to that of Mount Desert, as early explorers no doubt spied its shoreline and set foot on its soil. Indians from the area, often called Tarrentines or Etchemins, used to hunt and fish on Mount Desert Island. There were early French colonies all over the area. The land that was granted to Antoine De La Mothe Cadillac included part of what is now the town of Hancock, and there are remains of an early French settlement in the neighboring town of Franklin. During the American Revolution, men from both Mount Desert Island and the town of Sullivan were listed together on the militia pay rosters.

The first English settlers obtained the titles to their lands from Massachusetts, just as did the first settlers on Mount Desert Island, and at about the same time. In 1766, Philip and S. Hodgkins came from Georgetown, in the Province of Maine. Shortly afterward, Agreen Crabtree, Oliver Wooster, Thomas Googins, Thomas and James McFarland and Reubin and Moses Abbot followed, according to Coolidge and Mansfield. In addition, Thomas Moon, Francis Grant, William Gatcomb, James Smith, John Cook and Richard Clark also came and settled with their families.

Farming, fishing, lumbering, shipbuilding and coasting were among the pursuits of those who made their home in Hancock. According to George Varney in his 1886 *Gazetteer of the State of Maine*, there was one mill manufacturing staves, shingles and long lumber and one producing staves and short lumber. It is interesting that Varney, in his description of Hancock, also makes a point of stating that "there is a marked neatness about the buildings which tells of industry and thrift." This certainly cannot be considered merely incidental because at about the same time Samuel Wasson, in his 1878 *Survey of Hancock County*, reports of the town of Hancock, "A very noticeable feature is the absence of that *clutteration* which disfigures so many farm door yards."

There seems to be a residue of that "neatness" still about in the town of Hancock today. Rather than simply sort through musty papers and faded folders, I wanted to get a feel for the community by taking a look around. The stark white homesteads exuded a Spartan, no-nonsense feel that seemed to include a general tidiness. As I drove past each farmhouse, I found the fields and barns neatly kempt, as if they were still waiting for the horses to return. Indeed, Hancock appears as if it has not yet completely emerged from the nineteenth century or, in the very least, as though time is moving ahead as slowly as possible there.

Back at the historical society, I stood staring at the rows and rows of books and pamphlets.

"What can I tell people about the town of Hancock that hasn't already been written?" I asked Lois.

"Well, most people don't know about John Peck," she answered. "He had a store right here on Peck's Point."

John Peck, considered by many to have been America's first naval architect, was born in Boston in 1725 and educated as a merchant. A little-known fact, however, is that Mr. Peck ran a store in Sullivan, Maine, at a location that is now part of the town of Hancock, known as Peck's Point.

While still in school, John became interested in ship design, even venturing out to sea a few times as a young man in order to gain firsthand experience. During the American Revolution, in Watertown, Massachusetts, he was appointed inspector of saltpetre, an essential ingredient in gunpowder. Peck eventually put his "hobby" of shipbuilding to work as well.

Although Peck was a merchant by trade, he designed many sailing vessels during the Revolution, some quite famous. The brig *Hazard*, for instance, was built in Boston in 1777 and carried sixteen guns. Thomas Clark commented on the *Hazard* in his 1814 *Naval History of the United States.* "This vessel," he wrote, "proved to be one of the best and most elegant models ever built." Although the *Hazard* was successful, she was short-lived. In 1779, during the ill-fated Penobscot Expedition, the *Hazard* was burned on the Penobscot River to prevent her from falling into British hands.

The *Empress of China*, designed by Peck and built in Boston in 1783, is noted for being the first vessel to arrive in China under American colors. The *Empress of China* was also noted for being a fast sailer, as were many of Peck's vessels. The privateer *Belisarius*, for instance, was "reconed one of the fastest sailing ships that swam the Sea's," according to Joshua Humphrey Jr., designer of the *Constitution*, as related in Carl Cutler's *Greyhounds of the Seas.* Peck can also claim the honor of designing the first American vessel to be built abroad. The *Maréchal de Cartries* was built in France about 1782. Among other ships Peck is believed to have designed are the *Protector*, a twenty-eight-gun frigate, and the speedy privateer *Rattlesnake.*

John Peck's attitude is likely what has prevented him from gaining the recognition that he deserves. It appears that he was often argumentative and egotistical, tending to alienate some of those with whom he interacted. He was also secretive and "easily discouraged," according to Howard Chapelle in his *History of American Sailing Ships*. Leander Bishop remarked in his 1861 *History of American Manufacturers*:

> *The ships built by him were so superior to any then known, that they attracted the attention of Congress, and he was employed to build some of their ships of war. But his talents did not bring him that pecuniary reward which all who knew the superiority of his skill, have admitted was his due.*

Although John Peck didn't receive the esteem that might have been due him, his son, William Dandridge Peck, was a noted Harvard professor as well as that university's first entomologist. With the exception of the speedy ships that John Peck designed, not very much is known of him.

If one ventures to Hancock, Maine, and visits the Hancock Historical Society, however, there is somewhat more to be learned. There is a copy of an eighteenth-century bill of lading stating that the goods described are

> *shipped by the Grace of God, in good order and well conditioned, by John Peck, in and upon the good schooner called the* Black Snake *whereof is Master, under God, for this present Voyage, John Patterson, and now riding at Anchor in the Harbor of Boston and by God's Grace bound for Frenchmens Bay.*

The bill of lading, dated November 23, 1771, lists the following merchandise:

> *One Barrell Rum, Two Barrells Molasses, Twenty Four Barrells Indian Meal, One Barrell Beef, One barrel Pork, Six Tin Lamps, 1 doz horn combs, Eleven Ivory Combs, Three doz and a half of Tea Spoons, Fifteen Striped Blankets, Three Tan'd Seal Skins.*

Another bill of lading lists more items shipped on the schooner "*Black Snake* for Frenchman's Bay," also dated November 23, 1771:

> *Shears, shoe jacks, best French flints, pidgeon shot, goose shot, duck shot, shoe tacks, hand pots, large pots, wine, cotton, Irish linen, worsted caps, broad India ribbons, sq pointed jack knives, sharp pointed knives.*

The last sentence on the paper reads, "And so God send the good Schooner to her desired Port in safety, Amen. Dated in Boston, Nov. 23. 1771," and this document is signed by the master of the *Black Snake*, "Jon Paterson."

So in the very least we know what folks Down East wanted from Boston in the latter part of the eighteenth century, but perhaps more importantly, we can get a feel of the significance of shipping itself. Sailing vessels were a lifeline to modern society, as well as a way of life, and the sea was interwoven into the fabric of everyday existence. Ships seemed to have taken on their own personalities and were clearly considered more than merely objects in which to travel on the sea. It was as if the vessels' very timbers absorbed some element of each journey, each hardship on the sea and perhaps some trace of each crew member as well.

There were thirty-eight vessels built in Hancock; most of them were schooners, and a few were brigs. There were also many ships built in nearby towns that were operated by Hancock people. Hancock is more famous for its

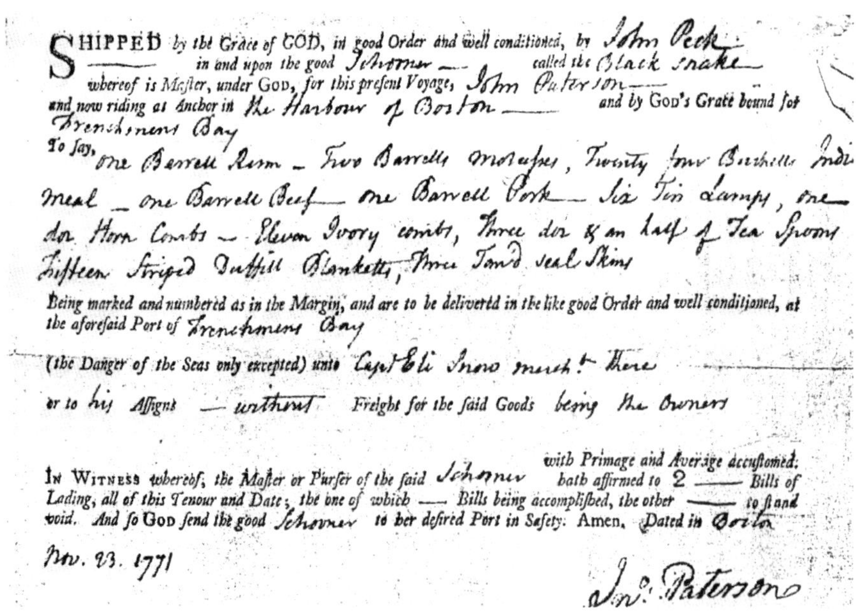
SHIPPED by the Grace of GOD, in good Order and well conditioned, by John Peck in and upon the good Schooner called the Black Snake whereof is Master, under GOD, for this present Voyage, John Paterson and now riding at Anchor in the Harbour of Boston and by GOD's Grace bound for Frenchmens Bay

To say, one Barrell Rum – Two Barrells molasses, Twenty four Bushells Indi meal – one Barrell Beef – one Barrell Pork – Six Tin Lamps, one doz Horn Combs – Eleven Ivory combs, Three doz & an half of Tea Spoons Fifteen Striped Duffill Blanketts, Three Tann'd seal Skins

Being marked and numbered as in the Margin, and are to be delivered in the like good Order and well conditioned, at the aforesaid Port of Frenchmens Bay (the Danger of the Seas only excepted) unto Capt Eli Snow merch.t there or to his Assigns – without Freight for the said Goods being the Owners with Primage and Average accustomed: In Witness whereof, the Master or Purser of the said Schooner hath affirmed to 2 Bills of Lading, all of this Tenour and Date; the one of which Bills being accomplished, the other to stand void. And so GOD send the good Schooner to her desired Port in Safety: Amen. Dated in Boston Nov. 23. 1771

Jno. Paterson

Bill of lading for John Peck cargo on the schooner *Black Snake* from Boston sailing for Frenchman's Bay. *Courtesy of the Hancock Historical Society.*

shipmasters than its ships, however. Seafaring stories are multitudinous and spring from every letter, logbook, newspaper article and personal recollection.

The story of the brig *Homeward Bound* is certainly interesting, and it was found in an envelope with many other seafaring stories at the historical society. The information was likely originally obtained from letters, journals or even personal recollections. This story was told by Augustus Foss, who was born in Hancock in 1838 and later killed in the Civil War. The words "Last Voyage of the Brig *Homeward Bound*, by Jack Windard" are typewritten on the first page.

We begin with a sailor whom we believe to be Augustus Foss, who ends up on board the *Homeward Bound* acting as second mate. It is unclear from the document exactly what the time period is, but we know it is autumn, sometime before the Civil War. Since there is a reference to the "South Shoal Lightship" off Nantucket in the story, we know the events take place after June 15, 1854, as that is when the lightship was established.

"I had finished a trip to the west coast of Africa in the bark *Sunshine* taking over a cargo of New England rum," the sailor relates. The return cargo for New York included olive oil, wood and gum. "A few of us stayed by to make another trip, but after she was discharged it was found necessary to make some repairs and the owners ordered her to her home port."

The brig's home port was Portland, and Augustus eventually traveled to Portland but did not find the ship there. Instead, he found only a few schooners that would be working the coast during the winter, and "having no desire for that I took the boat back to Boston."

In Boston, Augustus looked everywhere for a vessel to ship on, and clearly he would have liked a passage to someplace warmer than the New England coast. He made his way to Battery Wharf, where he found Hancock captain Henry Wooster and his first mate, John Stover, preparing to row out to the vessel *Homeward Bound*.

"Seeing me coming down the wharf," Augustus explained, "they gave me the typical Down East hail of 'Hello Gus, whither away?'" To which he replied, "Just taking in the sights, Captain Hen," and said he was looking for work but had not yet found any.

"Then why don't you put your dunnage on board the old brig?" Captain Wooster asked, explaining that he would first be going back to Franklin, Maine, to load box shooks and hogshead staves for St. Domingo in the West Indies. "The crew are home boys from Hancock and Ellsworth. We are chartered on logwood back to Boston," Captain Wooster added.

A horse and driver wait patiently at a wharf in Maine. The horse is wearing winter shoes with cleats, and behind his collar there is a folded blanket. *Author's collection.*

"This came near causing me to deny, as I did not care to come north of Cape Cod in the winter. But I never had much money to give a boarding master so decided to go," the sailor explained.

After making necessary preparations, Augustus Foss found a boatman to row him out to the brig, which was "laying on East Boston flats." He arrived aboard the *Homeward Bound* about five o'clock in the evening, spending most of the autumn night on the forecastle head, "smoking and singing the old ocean chanteys." He was clearly enjoying the time he was spending with his crewmates, happy to ship with folks he knew on a Maine vessel.

"Next morning we got underway and had a nice little run down by Thatcher's and across to Mt. Desert Rock and up into Frenchman's Bay," Foss related. The cargo at Franklin was ready to go, and "we made quick work of loading the old hooker."

The local sailors took advantage of the light southerly breeze that held their vessel at Sullivan Harbor for a week, providing the opportunity to spend a few nights at home. Eventually, we learn that "a fine northwest wind ran us out of the bay and off shore and we had a fine run to and past Hatteras."

After passing the coast of North Carolina, the *Homeward Bound* and her contingent of Hancock County seafarers met with one gale after another, relentlessly pounding the vessel as regularly occurs aboard sailing ships during these bouts with foul weather. And then things got worse, much worse, as the *Homeward Bound* sailed farther south. It is not clear how these Maine sailors contracted yellow fever in the West Indies, but half the crew was lost to the malady.

"I am not sure how or in what way we reached Turks Island. I am sure not one of us were rational at all times," Augustus Foss said. The Maine sailors remained at Turks Island for twenty days, "cared for by an English doctor."

Unfortunately, the *Homeward Bound* never made it back to Boston with the load of logwood. The sailors "had a good run up around Hatteras," and the brig made it as far as Cape Cod when it met with "the gale" near the South Shoal Lightship off Nantucket.

"After all our troubles it seemed hard to think the *Homeward Bound* should lay her bones on Cape Cod," Augustus Foss stated.

Luckily for Foss and the remaining crew members, the lifesaving crew from Nantucket was able to rescue all the men aboard the brig. Eventually,

Crabtree's Store and the post office, Hancock, Maine. Taken sometime in the 1920s. *Courtesy of the Hancock Historical Society.*

they made their way back to Maine. This has been just one story in many that I found at the historical society in Hancock.

What better way to learn of history than to read it in the words of those who experienced it? These are not the words of scholars, wealthy men or celebrated people; these are the words of everyday folks. These are people who put forth their best effort to endure hardship, people who lived, loved and perished meeting many of the same challenges that we do today. It is as close as we can get to conversing with ghosts, connecting with the past and getting a glimpse of what day-to-day life was like in times and places other than our own. Perhaps someday our own words will be read in a book of history.

One does not generally think of coastal Maine when contemplating the American Civil War, but perhaps we should. Maybe in the twenty-first century we need to realize what an all-encompassing thing this nineteenth-century conflict really was and the toll it took on families everywhere.

Following, we see a letter written by Helen Graves Crabtree during the Civil War, or the War of the Rebellion, as it was known at the time, and this particular letter was written the day after Christmas. Helen was worried that her husband, George, who was working out of town, would be drafted and

John Springer Sr. and his team in Hancock, 1918. *Courtesy Hancock Historical Society.*

killed. In Helen's letter we also find a reference to Augustus Foss, the sailor who survived the last voyage of the *Homeward Bound*:

> *Hancock, Dec. 26, 1862*
> *My Dear Husband*
> *I thought I could not spend a portion of this evening in a more pleasant manner than in writing to you.*
>
> *Poor Joe Cline is dead. He died at Yorktown, poor fellow. They are going to have his remains home, they feel very badly about him, I pitty them, he has been sick ever since he went away. The climet did not agree with him. Agustus Bragdon of Franklin got as far as Ellsworth and died thare and a Mr. Orcut got home Monday and died at four the next morning. He left a family. Lymon Wests boy is dead. Leonard Higgins is dead and is to be buerried tomorrow. Agustus Foss is dead poor fellow. When will this dreadful war ceace. The war has caused a great many to mourn for friends.*
>
> *I have heard it said that this war would never stop til every family was to mourn and I do not know but it is so. It seems hard and unjust but God only knows his ways are not for us to know.*
>
> *I must close now, good night dearest one, write soon and a long letter.*
>
> *Your Helen.*

When we hear from Helen again, she is clearly distraught over her husband's continued absence and raising their baby daughter, Effie, on her own. She gives the reader a surprising insight into her thoughts about the war when she says, lamenting on the death of a friend, "He was too good to go out there and dye for nothing." Helen herself would be dead a few months after writing the following letter, succumbing to tragic illness. For a woman so concerned about misfortune befalling others, Helen did not seem to be aware of her own mortality:

> *Hancock, May 6, 1863*
> *My Dear Husband*
> *Your letter of the fourth I received to day and was very much supprised and dissappointed too for it had been so long since I had a letter from you I thought you was on your way home and was looking for you instead of a letter so you can judge of my dissappointment.*

How long do you think it will be before you come home? O I did want to see you very much. I want you to see little Effie she is so cunning. The other day I was looking at your picture and I showed it to her and told her to kiss Pappa and she kissed it ever so many times. She will kiss Issias doll every time she sees it but when we shut its eyes up she will cry.

I wish I had some news to write to you. I suppose you knew that poor Lenard Butler was dead. His remains were brought home and buerried last Monday. He died at Port Royal of ship fever and ended in conjestion of the brain poor fellow. He was too good to go out there and dye for nothing. He was a comfort to his family and an orniment to cociety but alas he is dead and how many more like him have we got to sacrifise before this horrid war is ended God only knows.

I have seen Dr. Harden he was here when Ed was sick. I like him first rate. He examined my lungs and gave me some cough medecine and only charged me 25cts. He says Ed is not fit to go to war he says it kneads strong able bodied men. Ed was threatened with lung fever. He is not well this spring he looks thin and pale.

I must close so good night dearest from your loving Helen.

As a footnote, Helen died on January 1, 1864, from consumption, or what we call tuberculosis today. Her husband was never drafted.

Soldiers from Maine, brave and dedicated, fought for the United States in many wars. The First World War, or the War to End All Wars, as it was so often called, was no exception. Harold Foss from Hancock and Walter Farnsworth were both lieutenant commanders on the USS *Hilton*, which carried desperately needed troops and supplies overseas during the war. Walter Farnsworth is the author of a letter written to folks back home while he was in Quiberon Bay, France, just after the end of the war. The letter was published in a January 1919 edition of the *Ellsworth American* entitled "Down East Skippers Put the Stuff Across":

Just a few lines from one of Maine's native sons who tried to uphold the traditions for which the "Old Pine Tree State" is proud, in this war with Kaiser Bill. Having completed fifteen months of service over here, I am naturally aching to get back to the good old U.S.A., but willing to stay and do my part so that the boys who are still over here will not miss anything that is in my power to bring them. I have been in command of the U.S.S.

> Hilton, *a 5,000 ton capacity ship, during my career on this side of the water, which has landed 100,000 odd tons of munitions and supplies to the boys in khaki, from the ports of America, England, Scotland, and Wales, to the West Coast of France, through the war zone, mostly through the treacherous English Channel where Kaiser Bill warned us to stay out of, and where he played so much havoc, but where finally he had to bow to Yankee prowess.*

Perhaps one of the most famous shipmasters from Hancock is Captain George Dow, the last master of the world's only seven-masted schooner, the *Thomas W. Lawson*. The *Lawson* went down near the Scilly Isles off Cornwall, Great Britain, after a stormy and arduous transatlantic passage in 1907.

The *Thomas W. Lawson* was built at the Fore River Ship and Engine Company in Quincy, Massachusetts, and launched on July 10, 1902. She was steel-hulled, her overall length was an astounding 475 feet and she was 50 feet wide. She was designed by Bowdoin B. Crowninshield, who was, strangely enough, a Harvard-educated designer of racing yachts. The *Lawson* was the largest commercial sailing vessel ever constructed for operation without an auxiliary engine. She was pure sailing ship and carried 43,000 square feet of canvas. Built to compete with the successful four-, five- and six-masted wooden-hulled schooners, whose hulls tended to sag or hog over time, a steel-hulled, seven-masted schooner seemed to make sense.

The *Lawson* didn't perform as well as expected, however. She was notoriously difficult to handle, tended to yaw and nearly capsized while lying at a dock in Sabine, Texas. To further complicate matters, the *Lawson*, with her thirty-two-foot draft, could not enter many ports loaded to capacity, nor could she always remain within sight of shore.

It would be the first time the gargantuan schooner would make a transatlantic trip, and nobody really knew how she would handle. Some postulate that her regular master, Captain Arthur Crowley, wasn't comfortable with the thought of a lengthy voyage in the as yet untested vessel, already known to be difficult to maneuver on shorter excursions. Whatever the reason, Captain George Dow from Hancock, Maine, was the shipmaster who took on this ultimately perilous mission, and the voyage was beset with difficulty from the start. Dow, at fifty-nine years of age, had quite an impressive record commanding large sailing ships, although it was said that he usually preferred square-rigged vessels.

Unfortunately, many blame Captain Dow for the eventual loss of the vessel, which has been considered by some to be the result of bad judgement. In all fairness to the Yankee skipper, however, Captain Dow had many obstacles to overcome before the journey even began. It had become increasingly difficult to find crews for sailing vessels, and it would seem that the *Lawson* had a bad reputation from the start; nobody wanted to sail on her. In addition, she had thirteen letters in her name, *Thomas W. Lawson*, and was already known as a "bad luck ship."

On November 19, 1907, when the *Lawson* departed from the Marcus Hook refinery in Pennsylvania loaded with two and a quarter million gallons of light oil for London, she ran aground and had to be pulled off a sandbank by a tugboat. Of her eighteen crew members, eleven were foreign and likely could not speak much English. The men before the mast were at best inexperienced. The first mate and engineer, however, were very competent and had experience sailing the large steel-hulled vessel.

Captain Dow's bad luck continued as the *Lawson* ran into three gales, damaging the ship's lifeboats and much of the equipment on deck and tearing many of her sails. In between the storms, the behemoth vessel was becalmed. By the time the schooner crossed the Atlantic, she was just off the notorious rock-strewn Isles of Scilly, southwest of Cornwall, England. It was Friday, December 13, 1907. The keepers of nearby Bishop's Rock Lighthouse sent up flares warning the crew of the *Lawson* of the imminent danger. Instead of attempting to extricate the vessel from its precarious position or considering abandoning ship, Captain Dow dropped the schooner's two anchors and did nothing. Unfortunately, Captain George Dow wasn't a superstitious fellow.

The huge schooner was lying amidst a labyrinth of treacherous rocks, many just below the surface. Hundreds of ships had been wrecked in this place, and Captain Dow certainly knew it. He also knew that cargoes were removed from abandoned vessels, and this provided the local mariners with a lucrative business. By the afternoon of Friday 13, two lifesaving crews in two boats made their way to the *Lawson* with difficulty, fighting rising seas and strong winds. Despite their efforts, Captain Dow would not relinquish his vessel and allow the lifesaving teams to remove his crew members. Instead, he insisted the *Lawson*'s anchors would hold. This fearless Yankee skipper would not give up his ship.

Sometime early the next morning, the *Thomas W. Lawson*'s two five-ton stockless anchors began to drag, succumbing to the force of the relentless winds and heavy seas. When the anchor chains broke, the schooner soon struck bottom, tore a hole in her hull and eventually split in two. Many of the crew, who had lashed themselves to the towering masts in order to escape the destructive seas below, became hopelessly tangled in the rigging when the giant masts fell into the ocean. Freezing rain and howling winds punished the men and what was left of their vessel. Words likely cannot describe the horror that ensued.

All but two of her crew of eighteen perished; the survivors were engineer Edward Rowe and Captain Dow. George Dow suffered severe injuries and was never the same. The fifty-eight thousand barrels of oil that spilled into the sea likely created the first large oil spill in history.

We can tell what most of contemporary society thought about the wreck of the *Thomas W. Lawson*, or sailing vessels in general, after reading an article from the January 1908 issue of the *Literary Digest* entitled "The Victory of Steam":

> *The wreck of the seven-masted American schooner* Thomas W. Lawson, *on Friday, the 13th of December, which is reported from England by the daily press is made the occasion for pointing out that the recent attempts to revive transportation by sailing vessels, in competition with steam, have not been successful. It has long been believed that the sailing vessel is doomed to extinction as a competitor for ocean freight transportation.*

It is no wonder that it was Captain Dow from Hancock who took over the *Lawson* on her first transatlantic voyage; he was a man who had faith in a sailing vessel. He believed in the old ways, and he was fearless. The Maine wind and sea had raised him, and he knew a sailing ship better than he knew anything else. Hancock has produced some of the best shipmasters in Maine and has built some fine vessels and provided the crews to sail them. The stories attached to some of these ships and their captains are numerous; the stories that have been left untold are likely countless.

It's more than shipmasters and shipping that distinguishes Hancock. Hancock does not owe all its sophistication to its neighbor in the west or even to the numerous summer folks who spent their time on Hancock Point. Since 1943, the Pierre Monteux School, an internationally renowned school for conductors and orchestra musicians, has made its home in Hancock. Although a seemingly unlikely spot amidst farmhouses, fields and gravel roads, the celebrated conductors' school still draws more than seventy students each year, and its reputation has never waned.

Acclaimed conductor Pierre Monteux was born in France in 1875 and became a citizen of the United States in 1942. He chose Hancock, Maine, as the location of his school because it was the childhood home of his wife, Doris Hodgkins Monteux. Coincidentally, the Monteux School is located on land that was once owned by Madame Bacler de Leval, who fled to America to escape the French Revolution. Madame de Leval purchased her property from Madame de Gregoire and planned to establish a center of French culture in the area. It is ironic that, centuries later, Monteux chose that location for his school. At the time of his death in 1964, Pierre Monteux was the primary conductor for the London Symphony Orchestra.

To the astute observer, Hancock's true value really lies in its people rather than its proximity to Bar Harbor. Many of these people are somewhat famous in their own right and others not at all. It is the combination of many talented people throughout its history that makes Hancock such a varied and interesting coastal Maine community, even today. It is the traditional

Captured in time, these faces stare back at us from the Hancock Grange Fair that was held on September 27, 1914. The building in the background is the town hall. *Courtesy Hancock Historical Society.*

American village that we all yearn to come home to, where there are still honest, decent folk who know their roots and keep their history close by.

Before I left Hancock, I asked Lois what the sign heading into town that read "Carrying Place" was all about.

"It's just a marshy place, between the Taunton River on one side and the sea on the other. A place where you had to get off your horse and then be carried across in a boat. It separates this part of town from the rest. Why would you want to know that?"

"Because I passed the sign coming in to town," I said. "After all these years somebody must have thought it was important because they put the sign there. And where are those old railroad tracks? I couldn't find them anywhere."

"Well you didn't look very hard," Lois said, smiling and pointing out the window. "They are right out there across from this building, what's left of them."

I went outside and looked, but the tracks were gone. Instead, I found an overgrown pathway leading on into infinity, obscured by overgrowth and crowded with branches and bushes. A warm breeze tossed branches that were being illuminated by the afternoon sun. It was hard to believe this was once the most heavily traveled line on the Maine Central Railroad. The Bar Harbor Express Line has today become an obscure hiking trail in an almost unknown Maine village. The railroad has gone, but the legacy it has left will remain. The same is true for Hancock's maritime heritage, the vessels and the shipmasters. Although they have vanished materially from our realm of experience, they have taken their place in history and are worthy of reawakening once more.

CAPTAIN HAROLD FOSS

A Family of Seafarers

There are certainly many interesting shipmasters from Hancock, but the most famous is likely Captain Harold Foss. He is a man who kept sailing vessels, especially schooners, viable commercially throughout much of the twentieth century. Owner of the last fleet of windjammers to ply the Atlantic, this is a man who nearly single-handedly forestalled the end of an era. This is a man who changed the course of maritime history on the East Coast.

During a time when horses were being put out to pasture, carriages put up in haylofts and old schooners run aground to rot in rivers and along wharfs, Foss went out looking for sailing ships to recondition and put back to sea.

"If I had fifty sailing vessels I could put them all to work," he was often quoted as saying. Foss deplored the practice of running the large ships aground to eventually rot away.

"Recently, three or four vessels could still have been brought back if any possibility of making a profit with them could have been seen," he told a reporter from the *Lewiston Sun* in 1937. "But the present demand came too late. They are now beyond repair."

Harold Foss was born in Hancock, Maine, on April 10, 1881, early enough to get a glimpse of the age of sail in all its glory. His father and grandfather were shipmasters, and if the blood that flows through our veins can shape us, Foss is certainly a fine example. In a 1934 interview with the *Brooklyn Daily Eagle*, Foss describes his early seafaring experiences:

Above: Schooners in Miami during the land boom, carrying lumber and building materials. This photo, taken in 1925, shows many of the Maine schooners that were still in service at the time. The second vessel is the famous four-master *Luther Little* that was aground in Wiscasset for over sixty years. *From the Foss Collection, courtesy of the Penobscot Marine Museum.*

Right: Captain Harold Foss. *Courtesy of the Hancock Historical Society.*

A sea of masts, these mostly square-rigged vessels are lying at docks along South Street in New York City, taking on and discharging their cargoes, about 1880. *Author's collection.*

> *Many a time when I was a kid I walked along South Street, New York, with my father, who was then master and managing owner of the schooner* John Paul. *Father showed me hundreds of large square-riggers loading for various parts of the world.*

Harold's father, Captain Orlando Foss, was also a well-known shipmaster and successful businessman. After his career as shipmaster ended, he went into the banking business, eventually becoming a bank president and also a member of the Maine legislature. There were three schooners built in Franklin, Maine, for Orlando Foss. These were the *W.H. Card* built in 1874, the *Annie E. Rickerson* built in 1881 and the tern schooner *John Paul* built in 1891.

The *W.H. Card* has an interesting story attached to it, and it begins in 1879, when the vessel was under the command of Orlando Foss's cousin, Captain Almus Foss, and had a crew of five. Bringing a cargo to Haiti, the *W.H. Card* was relentlessly pounded by gale after gale and lost all the water casks that had been secured on the deck. There was not much water stored below deck, and what there was didn't last very long. Having little choice, the crew had to refill the remaining casks with water from a river in Haiti and drink that. When they finally made their destination, Cap-Haïtien, they discharged their cargo and then headed for Port Liberte to load logwood for New York.

As the *W.H. Card* headed northward, she was again met with gale after gale, and then her crew became very sick. It was the dreaded Haitian fever. Two of the five men eventually died, and the others became very ill, with the exception of the captain and mate, who were strangely unaffected. Unable to properly work the vessel without enough hands on deck during the turbulent weather, the schooner's fate was uncertain, and she likely rolled and pitched in the high seas, left to her own devices.

Sixteen days later, after the storms subsided and the *Card* neared Bermuda, she was drifting helplessly. When several boatmen from Bermuda sighted the craft, they approached her, and climbing aboard, one of them took the wheel and asked where the crew was. The captain answered by stating that one crew member was dead below and that the others were too sick to work. Realizing that fever was on the vessel, the boatmen quickly headed back to their boat, which was tied up alongside the schooner. At this point, Captain Almus Foss pulled out a revolver and threatened to shoot the first man who left his vessel. He is reputed to have said something like: "The first man who goes over that rail will take a piece of lead in his carcass!"

This Yankee skipper certainly knew that the only way his schooner would get into any port would be with a crew to sail her. Once they made Hamilton, Bermuda, the sick men were brought to a hospital there and eventually recovered. Captain Almus Foss found another crew in Bermuda and brought the *W.H. Card* safely home to Maine.

The *W.H. Card* eventually went down in December 1901. Frank Lowell from Bucksport, Maine, was master, and he planned to sail from Bangor, Maine, to Wareham, Massachusetts, and thought it should take two days. He had a crew of three men. Expecting a pleasant trip on the little schooner, Captain Lowell also brought his bride of only a few weeks and her sister along with him. It must have seemed like a wonderful, romantic idea to the young captain. On the first day out, a fierce nor'easter came from nowhere, tearing the mainsail away from its fastenings and tossing it into the rising sea. The heavy seas punished the vessel so badly that the pounding broke the steering gear, leaving the schooner to drift helplessly farther out into the ocean. After everything on deck was washed away, the ship began to leak badly. The drinking water casks were washed overboard, and the seas poured into the cabin and spoiled the provisions. Two weeks later, a steamer rescued them, with one of the crew seriously injured. Captain Lowell was resolved to finish his honeymoon on "some inland excursion," according to an article from the *New York Times*.

Harold Foss grew up hearing stories such as these. He accompanied his father aboard the *John Paul*, making his first journey when he was twelve, escorted by his mother. It didn't take young Harold very long to learn seamanship from his father and the experienced crew members aboard the *Paul*.

When the *John Paul* was launched in 1891, Harold Foss recalled in a 1963 interview with Isabel Currier for *Down East* magazine:

> *I was ten years old when Father and John Paul Gordon built the* John Paul *at Franklin, Maine, and the only way he could keep me off her was to lock me up at home or drive off to the shipyard before I was awake in the morning.*

The tern schooner *John Paul* was Harold Foss's first command when he was just nineteen years old. Their cargo was missionary supplies for the African Gold Coast—the reader may be interested to know exactly what those "missionary supplies" were.

"For my first command I took the schooner *John Paul* out of Boston with a cargo of rum and bibles for missionaries in Africa," Foss told a reporter from the *Montreal Gazette* in 1946.

In a letter written to his brother in 1963, Harold Foss described the man who built the *John Paul*:

> *John Paul Gordon was one of the 49ers. He came back to his home, Franklin, after the Civil War. He was a hail fellow well met, quite a competent man handling his liquor, liked ships and women. Besides he always had plenty of money.*

After making a few trips to Africa in the *Paul*, Foss moved on to larger vessels. He did whatever he needed to do to get the job done. While in command of the *Pendleton Satisfaction*, Captain Foss performed surgery at sea on a crew member who had broken bones protruding through the flesh in his leg.

The *Sallie C. Marvil. From the Foss Collection, courtesy of the Penobscot Marine Museum.*

The *Sallie C. Marvil* was the first four-master that Foss commanded, and with her he had many adventures. His daring rescue at sea of another schooner in 1910 is certainly interesting. In November 1910, when Foss was skipper of the *Sally C. Marvil*, she was loaded with a cargo of lumber. He was nearing Cape Lookout, off the coast of North Carolina, and with seas becoming rough, a crew member on the *Marvil* noticed a ship in the distance with her ensign flying upside down, a signal of distress. Turning the *Marvil* into the wind to slow her down and get a closer look at the disabled vessel, Foss recognized it as the schooner *Florence Shay*. The master of the *Shay* recognized Captain Foss and yelled across to him that his ship was sinking.

Foss answered back, telling the *Shay*'s captain to take in the foresail and saying that he would stand by with the *Marvil.* With the seas becoming rougher and the weather generally unfavorable and getting worse, Foss didn't think he could launch his yawl boat, but of course he was determined to save the crew. Upon hearing the *Shay* was loaded with a lucrative cargo—paving stones—Foss was determined to save the vessel and cargo as well.

After several attempts to get a towline to the *Shay*, the *Marvil*'s crew was finally successful, but the line broke and the vessel and crew were again at the mercy of the raging seas. An old trick used to temporarily ease rough seas is to create an oil slick near your vessel, which Foss did. As a last resort, he ordered the crew to dump oil to the windward, which smoothed the seas enough to get the yawl boat to the other vessel and bring her crew back to the safety of the *Marvil*. After rescuing Captain Gilbert and the crew of the *Shay*, Foss made sure the hungry men had their fill of baked beans and brown bread.

Salvaging the *Shay* and her cargo would not be so easy. By this time, the damaged schooner was about a mile to the leeward and rolling badly. Foss sent three men over to the vessel in the yawl boat to pump her out, but when they got to her, the rough seas smashed their small boat into pieces. Luckily, they managed to climb aboard the sinking schooner and begin their work. On the *Marvil*, Foss was improvising, making a new towline out of the wire topping lifts from the *Marvil*'s four masts and shackling them together. After the weather improved, Foss was able to sail the *Marvil* close enough to the *Shay* to throw a rope across, which was attached to the wire cable. When the towing line was made fast to the *Shay*, the men raised her sails in order to take pressure off the line so it wouldn't break again. Then, Captain Foss set the *Marvil*'s sails and began towing the disabled schooner back into port. He and his crew shared the salvage money, their efforts paying off with a very nice bonus in pay.

Unfortunately, the time when one might have personally interviewed Captain Foss has passed, just as his beloved schooners have all but passed from our range of experience. Luckily, the scope of all that he has accomplished was so great that others were stirred to commemorate his achievements. There are numerous news articles, letters, photographs and people who remember him. It is from this wealth that we can draw.

In a drawer at the historical society, there was a folder filled with letters from Harold Foss, the following one just prior to his rescue of the *Florence Shay*:

> *Savannah, Ga.*
> *Oct. 22, 1910*
>
> *Dear Father:*
> *Your letter was received this morning. We are continually hearing news of more disaster from the hurricane.* [This severe hurricane would be considered a category four by today's standards]. *Glad to see Capt.* [George W.] *Dow has got back to Tampa. Soon as I arrived here I wired to Mr. Herssey in Jacksonville and asked for the "Paul." He wired*

back she had not arrived. I have been looking anxiously for tidings of her, for I know she has had a hard time. It blew at Tyber 90 miles per hour. She was off Frying Pan [the Frying Pan Shoals are located off Cape Fear in North Carolina and have long been considered treacherous] *when I was close to Lookout* [Cape Lookout, North Carolina]. *We made about six miles per hour from there here and I thought she might have reached Jax. The water here came just to the top of the wharf. Every vessel was made fast in good shape.*

Expect to finish discharging Tuesday. Rutledge finishes today. He is going to Belfast [Maine] *to load for Perth Amboy. They chartered the "Antioch" to load the "goatina" in Venezuela for New haven.*

Suppose you are busy with apples, etc.

See our namesake is nominated for Governor of Mass [Eugene Foss was elected forty-fifth governor of Massachusetts, taking office on January 4, 1911].

The *John Paul* badly damaged off the Florida coast in September 1897. The schooner was headed from Brunswick, Georgia, to New York with a cargo of lumber and was driven as far south as St. Augustine, Florida, in a storm. *From the Foss Collection, courtesy of the Penobscot Marine Museum.*

Will write again before leaving and shall also look for letters, your son, Harold.

Clearly, Foss was worried about his beloved tern schooner. The *John Paul* did not go down, however, until January 13, 1914, during a storm off Cape Cod. The wreck of the schooner was located on August 11, 1979, when two divers near the Nantucket ship channel found her remains. They reported the hull intact and that the load of granite the vessel was carrying from Stonington, Maine, to New York was still on board.

Many of the last commercial sailing vessels afloat during the twentieth century belonged to Foss & Crabtree and were the direct result of the entrepreneurial savvy of Captain Harold Foss. In the interview with Isabel Currier, Harold Foss explained:

Captain Fred Crabtree and I were a couple of Hancock boys who owned our own ships and used them to carry our own cargoes, which is why we could afford to sail 'em long after steam had forced most sailing freighters into retirement.

The most famous of Foss's fleet of windjammers, those he sailed well into the twentieth century, happened to be the last five-masted schooner ever built.

Foss's much-loved *Edna Hoyt* following launching on December 11, 1920, in Thomaston, Maine. The note written in pencil on the back of the photo reads, "Approaching wharf to let people off." *Author's collection.*

"She was the last canvas-bedecked lady love in my life," Harold Foss recalled. He was speaking of the *Edna Hoyt*, a wooden-hulled, oversized merchant sailing vessel that many would argue was outdated years before she was built. But she was more than that, much more, and Foss knew it. He would keep her afloat as long as he could.

Between his roles as shipmaster and entrepreneur, Harold Foss found the time to serve his country in not one but *both* world wars, commanding transport ships. His record of service was spotless, and he was clearly a man who was good at everything he did.

Captain Foss enjoyed reading as well as writing. His 1964 article in the *American Neptune*, as well as an unpublished manuscript on Foss family genealogy, was among the treasures I found in the archives at the Hancock Historical Society. In addition to these, Harold Foss was a regular contributor to the *Ellsworth American*, writing a column about locally built sailing vessels.

After reading the newly released historical novel *Lydia Bailey*, by popular Maine-born author Kenneth Roberts (who lived in Kennebunkport near Pulitzer Prize–winning novelist Booth Tarkington), Captain Foss found some

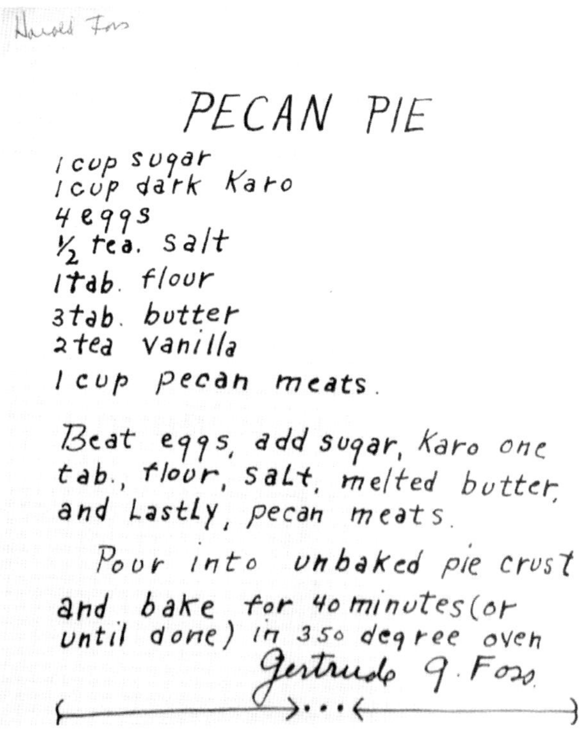

Harold Foss

PECAN PIE

1 cup sugar
1 cup dark Karo
4 eggs
½ tea. salt
1 tab. flour
3 tab. butter
2 tea vanilla
1 cup pecan meats.

Beat eggs, add sugar, Karo one tab., flour, salt, melted butter, and Lastly, pecan meats.

Pour into unbaked pie crust and bake for 40 minutes (or until done) in 350 degree oven

Gertrude G. Foss

Harold Foss's favorite pie? *Courtesy of the Hancock Historical Society.*

discrepancies in the work. In a letter dated March 10, 1947, Harold Foss wrote to Mr. Roberts from Liverpool, England:

> *Dear Mr. Roberts:*
>
> *During this voyage from New Orleans to this port of Liverpool I read* Lydia Bailey. *Like* Arundel *and* Oliver Wiswell *the moment that one sticks his nose into the book, he can't take it out until the book is finished. Consequently I neglected my Navigation and other important duties while I read the book. Upon finishing the book I put it in the ship's library and now the entire crew are eating it up.*
>
> *I made the remark to one of the officers that you did not go through the Hole in the Wall or around Abaco* [an island group in the Bahamas] *and the Isaac's on your way to Hayti as you say you did on page 70. For many years I was master of Maine schooners trading to Hayti and the other West India islands, and we never even considered such a thing as being caught West of Crooked Island passage. I can't find anywhere where Columbus ever sighted Abaco either. Now if you will jog up your memory I think you will find that you went down thru Caicos Passage in the* Hope *on your trip to Cap Francois; because nothing that ever wore canvas could beat from the Isaac's up to anywhere in Hayti. My mates are still arguing about this feat. After King Dick bought the cargo of rum in Cuba and you were on your way to Gibralter, that you did sight the Hole in the Wall or Abaco is possible; but you were probably in the Lee Scuppers with Lydia at that time and did not even think about navigation.*
>
> *Many times in Port au Prince I have seen the statue of General Toussaint* [former slave and early military leader of the Haitian Revolution] *but have never seen one of Christophe in all Hayti.* [Henri Christophe was a former slave and military leader who helped win Haiti independence from France in 1804, eventually becoming king of Haiti in 1811.] *I was told in Cap Hayti that he committed suicide by shooting himself with a silver bullet. I know that you have no time to answer these letters from your millions of readers, but I certainly would like to know if Christophe did use a silver bullet for that act.*
>
> *Very truly yours,*
> *Harold Foss*
> *Hancock, Maine*

Portland Head Light, located at Cape Elizabeth, Maine, sits at the entrance of Casco Bay and was first lit in 1791. *Photo by April Rossi.*

Cape Neddick or "Nubble" Lighthouse was constructed in 1879 and stands on Nubble Island at the entrance of the York River, York, Maine. *Photo by April Rossi.*

The four-masted *Margaret Todd* at her home port of Bar Harbor, against the backdrop of a surreal sunset. *Photo by April Rossi.*

The sun sets at Bass Harbor on Mount Desert Island. The Bass Harbor Head Light was first lit in 1858. *Photo by April Rossi.*

A passage back in time; the schooner *Mary Day* as seen from the starboard rail of the *Lewis R. French* in August 2011. *Photo by author.*

View of the sun setting aboard the schooner *Lewis R. French*, anchored just off Deer Isle, Maine. *Photo by author.*

The *Thomas W. Lawson*, the world's only seven-masted schooner, as depicted in a 1907 print. *Author's collection.*

The schooner *Victory Chimes* anchored off an uninhabited island in Penobscot Bay. *Photo by author.*

The schooner *Angelique* shares Merchants Row with a modern craft. *Photo by author.*

A map of the New World created in 1570, depicting Norumbega near the coast of Maine.

Left: Jedidiah Morse, author of *The American Universal Geography*, painted by his son, Samuel Finley Breese Morse, circa 1810. *Courtesy of the Yale University Art Gallery.*

Below: The schooner *Timberwind* near the Fox Islands, which were first named by Martin Pring in 1603. *Photo by author.*

Just off Camden Harbor, a race between schooners begins. It is June 2011. The vessels pictured are, from left: the *Olad*, an unidentified schooner in the distance, the *Stephen Taber* (black hull) and the *Lewis R. French* (gray hull). *Photo ©Craig S. Milner.*

The schooner *Stephen Taber* underway, her bow cutting through the seawater powered by a brisk wind. *Photo ©Craig S. Milner.*

Above: Victorious, the schooner *Stephen Taber* crosses the finish line and passes the Rockland Harbor Breakwater Light. *Photo ©Craig S. Milner.*

Left: The ship's bell aboard the schooner *Lewis R. French*. *Photo ©Craig S. Milner.*

Kenneth Roberts wasted no time in replying, and his letter was dated March 21, 1947:

> *Dear Captain Foss:*
> *You sea captains ought to tell me these things before books are published. How can I change 'em when you wait until about six editions have been run?*
> *I've heard that story about Christophe shooting himself with a silver bullet. This month's* Coronet, *annoyed at me because I wouldn't permit a digest of* Lydia Bailey, *tried to give me a backhanded slap by condensing John Vandercook's 20-year-old* Black Majesty, *which I enclose. In this it's said to be a gold bullet. Silver is the generally accepted yarn.*
> *Now about that trip to the southward. I was quoting from a letter written by one of my great, great grandfather's daughters. You'll find it quoted in* Trending Into Maine, *page 113.*
> *Since she called Eleuthera "Ethera" and made it Hole-in-the-Rock instead of Hole-in-the-Wall, she may have had defective vision as well. However, if you'll re-draft that passage, making it read as you think it ought to read from the viewpoint of a passenger on a brig in 1802, I'll see what I can do about getting the page replated.*
> *I forget where that thing about Columbus sighting Abaco came from, but I got it out of something that sounded pretty authoritative—maybe Morison, maybe Washington Irving—*somewhere, *certainly.*
> *Many thanks for the kind words.*
>
> *Sincerely,*
> *Kenneth Roberts*

Author Kenneth Roberts clearly had respect for Captain Foss's knowledge and sense of humor! Kenneth Roberts was born in Kennebunk, Maine, in 1885. He began his career working as a journalist for the *Saturday Evening Post*, for which he earned international acclaim. His historical novels became bestsellers, and he often received revision suggestions from his Pulitzer Prize–winning neighbor and friend Booth Tarkington.

Foss seems to have been a practical sort of fellow who only did the things that made sense to him and didn't change with the times unless it was advantageous to do so. As a master artisan knows the importance of keeping his tools in good condition, Foss knew that in order to succeed as shipmaster he needed to discipline his crew and maintain his vessel. In an interview with the *Montreal Gazette* in November 1946, Foss had this to say about his early seafaring experience: "In those days the better the discipline, the better the ship. Every ship master wanted to run a taut ship and keep her clean and pretty." Captain Foss later added, "The majority of seafaring men today are milk and water sailors, who prefer white shirts to white decks."

There were many witnesses to the condition of Harold Foss's ships. Francis Bowker, a sailor who later became a maritime author, had the following to say about his experience on the *Edna Hoyt* in his book *Blue Water Coaster*:

> *Though all these craft were old, there were some who were proud of the appearance their vessels made and strove to keep them seaworthy and sound. The five-master* Edna Hoyt *was kept in such spotless condition while I was in her in 1935 and 1936 that I heard a number of people inquire whether or not she was a yacht.*

In an interview with a reporter from the *Brooklyn Daily Eagle* in August 1934, Harold Foss remarked of the schooner *Edna Hoyt*, "I love that schooner. When it is a question of a new cover for a jib or a new suit of clothes for me, I clothe her first."

Later, he would succumb to his romantic notions of sailing vessels, especially Maine schooners, admitting in an interview with *Down East* magazine in September 1963:

> *If I could go to sea now, at eighty-one, by choice I'd be master of a sailing vessel. I don't mean a foreign-built bark, ship, or brig, like the stubby English ships with the jiboom cut off sharp or the square-sterned Scandinavians with a bow like the bad-toothed face of a wharf woman. I mean an American schooner, of the type built north of Cape Hatteras on the Atlantic seaboard, and especially in Maine, a lovely vessel full of grace, with long poles protruding above the rigging eyes, and a magnificent sheer, like the beautiful, stately carriage of any glamorous lady.*

A FORTUNE IN "GOATINA"

"A good ship is a paying ship," declared Captain Harold Foss early in his fifty-seven-year career at sea. Harold Foss did manage to make money with his beloved fleet of Maine schooners, despite the hardships imposed by the twentieth century and eventually a depression. During the 1930s, his several schooners were part of a group of just over a dozen windjammers still working the coastal routes on the Atlantic. All it took was a little bit of Yankee ingenuity and just plain common sense.

In 1909, Harold Foss was engaged in the molasses trade. Molasses was still a lucrative cargo for sailing vessels at the time, and Foss was quite happy in the business. The molasses was carried in hogsheads and barrels, which Foss picked up empty in Boston and carried by schooner to Puerto Rico, where they would be filled. A "hogshead" was a wooden cask, usually with a capacity for a "hogshead," which was also a liquid measure typically equivalent to sixty-three U.S. gallons. Before the advent of steam tankers, this was the way molasses was transported.

When loading the empty hogsheads or barrels in Boston, those placed on the lower tier were filled with water to be used as ballast for the outward journey, and the water was supposed to be dumped out in Puerto Rico. However, not all the water was dumped out in Puerto Rico, Foss later admitted, as it "did not hurt the molasses to have some water in it and it added to the merchant's profit."

Sometime in 1910, when Captain Foss was master of the four-masted schooner *Sallie C. Marvil* and his vessel was lying at a dock in Puerto Rico waiting to load a cargo of molasses for Boston, a random event occurred that changed the course of maritime history on the Atlantic. Another vessel, a dingy and unimpressive Venezuelan two-masted schooner, dropped anchor nearby. Eventually, Foss was approached by the master of the other schooner, as well as a man who was acting as business agent for both vessels. It would seem they wanted permission to tie the Venezuelan ship to the *Sallie C. Marvil*. In an article Foss wrote for the *American Neptune*, entitled "From Shipmaster to Guano Merchant," he described this event:

> *They asked if I had any objection to letting the schooner tie up alongside my vessel. As there existed among the sailing vessel masters a sort of fraternal spirit that was not apparent in steamships, of course I agreed that the other vessel could make fast to us though she was a disreputable-looking craft.*

Despite his initial apprehension, the Maine skipper succumbed to his good nature and invited the Venezuelan master aboard the *Sallie C. Marvil* and gave him a tour of the ship. Like a proud parent, Foss showed the Venezuelan his fancy master's accommodations, gave a basic tour of the vessel and ended by showing him the steam-powered winch. Obviously quite impressed, the Venezuelan admitted that he had never been aboard a four-masted schooner before. "I took a lot of pleasure in showing him around my modern vessel," Foss recalled, many years later.

After his tour of the *Sallie C. Marvil*, the master of the Venezuelan schooner asked Foss if he wouldn't mind taking some of his cargo on board for the business agent to inspect, as he was trying to sell it to him. Foss said he didn't mind but was surprised to find that the bags being carried onto his vessel contained goat manure.

By now the reader must have guessed what the "goatina" was. Fosse's euphemism "goatina" actually referred to goat manure or the Spanish word *guano*. The exportation of hides was a major business in Falcon, Venezuela, where the beat-up, two-masted schooner had come from. With many thousands of goats, all penned up in small corrals, the Venezuelan farmers were literally knee-deep in the stuff. Any relief from that encumbrance would certainly have been welcome.

The Venezuelan captain explained that the governor of the state of Falcon, Venezuela, owned his schooner. The governor was a young man named Leon Jurardo, who apparently had a good eye for business and hoped the guano might be sold for fertilizer in San Juan. Unfortunately, although the goat manure could be used to fertilize the sugar cane fields in Puerto Rico, the business agent wasn't prepared to pay very much for it. Consequently, the captain of the Venezuelan vessel, at Captain Fosse's suggestion, left fourteen bags of the stuff on the deck of the *Marvil* in hopes that it could be sold back in the States. Foss was a shrewd Yankee businessman and didn't want to pass up any opportunities to make some money. So Harold Foss left San Juan with a cargo of molasses for Boston and fourteen bags of "goatina" on the deck of his schooner.

When he arrived in Boston with the hogsheads of molasses, Foss got word that his brother Boyd had passed away and that his funeral had been held the day before. Naturally somewhat distraught, he completely forgot about the bags of goat manure sitting on the deck of his vessel and promptly returned to Hancock, Maine, to comfort his parents.

When Foss eventually returned to his schooner in Boston, he went down to Cape Ann, Massachusetts, to load paving stones for New York. In New York, he loaded a cargo for Savannah, Georgia, all this time with fourteen bags of goat manure on his schooner's deck. Not surprisingly, the crew was becoming annoyed with having to work around the bags of manure and began to protest. Consequently, while he was in Savannah, Foss asked his agent there if he knew of anybody who might be interested in buying a cargo of manure to use for fertilizer. The agent suggested he visit the American Agricultural Chemical Company located nearby and made an appointment for him.

Captain Foss kept the appointment and the following morning showed up at the American Agricultural Chemical Company with a small paper bag containing his sample of "goatina." What happened next is so startling that I will present it to the reader in Foss's own words, as written for the *American Neptune*:

> *Much to my astonishment, the plant superintendent took a good-sized mouthful of my sample and started chewing it thoroughly. After spitting it out, he said that it contained some ammonia but that it was worthless and that he could not use it.*

> *After that, I could not resist telling him that I was simply trying to introduce goat manure for fertilizing purpose and not as a source of food. This, however, did not cause him to change his mind.*

Although Foss wasn't successful selling his "goatina" in Savannah, he didn't give up completely. After a few trips up and down the eastern seaboard loading and discharging cargoes of lumber, Foss sailed the *Marvil* to Jacksonville, Florida, for yet another cargo of lumber. This time, when the ship was being towed up the St. Johns River, the first mate finally asked for permission to throw the fourteen bags of goat manure overboard. Foss asked him to wait until the vessel was on its way back down the river, and then he could dump it.

Clearly, Captain Foss knew what he was doing because shortly after the discussion with the mate, there appeared along the riverfront numerous fertilizer plants. After the disaster in Savannah, the Maine skipper knew he needed to carefully choose his next venture and picked the smallest, least pretentious fertilizer factory he saw. It happened to be the E.O. Painter Fertilizer Company, and that was where he took a cigar box filled with "goatina."

"He seemed interested, and he kept smelling the box of guano," Foss wrote later. After inviting the shipmaster to Sunday dinner at his mansion in Jacksonville, Mr. Painter eagerly agreed to try one cargo to see how it worked out. Of this dinner engagement, Foss wrote, "With my shoes shined and clothes pressed, I made my appearance at Mr. Painter's house. It was a mansion, and I enjoyed having dinner in such a lovely home."

Next, Captain Foss arranged to bring a load of coal down to Puerto Rico in the *Marvil* and then sailed to La Vela de Coro in Venezuela for the "goatina." He sailed at night, when the wind would be more suitable for his passage:

> *Crossing the Caribbean, the wind is always east during the daytime, and at nighttime it will be about east-northeast. Therefore as our course was south, we had the wind on our port beam; and for a four-masted schooner a beam wind is the best. She will sail fast and not make too much leeway.*

When the *Marvil* anchored near the port of La Vela de Coro, the customs officials came out to the vessel from shore. Foss was a man of the world and clearly knew how to handle himself in these situations. His ability to meet people on their own terms, as well as his charisma, certainly contributed to the advancement of this business venture. The reader will enjoy the skipper's own description of the event:

> *The custom of the country for these officials was to take a casual glance at the ship's papers, accept all cigars that the captain passed out, take a few drinks of whatever kind of liquor the captain offered, and then go back to shore. That settled all formalities until the ship was ready to clear.*

The next step was to go ashore and meet the governor, General Leon Jurardo, who was the mastermind behind the idea to use goat guano for fertilizer. It was likely that Foss was eager to meet Jurardo, probably seeing in him a kindred spirit. Although they were culturally worlds apart, history tells us that the two men got on famously. Jurardo was, according to Foss, "a tall, well-built man and looked more like a Yankee than a Spaniard."

During this time in history, South Americans were considered to be rather unscrupulous and not to be trusted, especially when dealing with entrepreneurs from the United States. The standing rule was simply not to trust them, and Foss knew it. Yet he was able to distinguish between this General Jurardo and the rest, clearly having a good eye for character, which is integral in successful business. The manuscript that Harold Foss wrote for his article in the *American Neptune* continued:

> *After crossing the Gulf Stream, the rule was to keep your eyes open and trust nobody. However, I soon found General Jurardo to be of a different stripe. We were friends for life, and I never heard of him doing anything unbecoming in any business deal.*

The only problem was that Jurardo spoke no English and Foss knew only a little Spanish. This situation was resolved in time but caused some problems initially. For instance, Foss noticed that nearly everybody he dealt with in La Vela de Coro carried a loaded revolver and a knife in his belt, including Jurardo. In order to promote good feelings, and "knowing that everybody likes presents," Foss decided to give the general his flashy pearl-handled revolver as a gift. Naturally, General Jurardo loved the pistol, but his translator told him that Foss wanted twenty dollars for it. Of course, Captain

Foss never saw the twenty dollars. The interpreter lost his job when the truth was revealed.

In order to ensure his success in the Venezuelan guano business, this Yankee skipper from Hancock, Maine, knew he had to learn a lot more about it. He was shrewd enough to know that he could not trust most of the locals and that they would likely rob him blind the first chance they got. With Jurardo as his guide, Foss spent a week traveling around Coro and visiting the goat farms on its outskirts. He must have felt like a fish out of water when he was told that the only way to get to the rural farms was by horseback: "I was not much of a rider, especially with the kind of saddle that I found out there. Still, the horses were tough old steeds; and I managed to see quite a lot of country."

Although the chief export in the region was goatskin, cheese was also made from goat milk. That added up to a lot of goats and therefore a lot of "goatina." Foss was convinced there was enough to keep him in business for quite a while, and there were already thousands of tons of the stuff waiting for shipment. It was the beginning of a very lucrative business that lasted nearly thirty years and put a lot of sailing vessels to work that would have otherwise lain idle at docks or rotted in riverbeds. By using the large Maine coastal schooners during much of the twentieth century, Captain Harold Foss single-handedly gave the age of sail a reprieve.

In 1917, when the United States entered World War I, Harold Foss joined the navy and was given the rank of lieutenant commander. After the Armistice in 1918, he got right back into the goat manure trade, this time also buying and shipping goatskin. Eventually, he expanded his Venezuelan cargoes to include products used in the tanning of leather and dyeing of cloth.

The Gulf Oil Company and Standard Oil Company chartered Foss's schooners to carry building materials and drilling equipment to Venezuela. Foss and Jurardo also cleverly sold some waterfront property that they had acquired to the Gulf Oil Company for a substantial profit. Foss even chartered a five-masted schooner, the *Edward B. Winslow*, to the Gulf Oil Company to bring materials out to Venezuela from Texas for construction of a pier and also to use as a warehouse and boardinghouse for the workmen. Not leaving any opportunity untested, Foss had the schooner's captain run a bar on the quarterdeck of the vessel; he "would have made a fortune," according to Foss, "if the poor devil could only have stayed on the sober side of the bar."

The schooner *Edward B. Winslow*, where Foss installed a bar to provide for the needs of thirsty sailors and workmen. *Author's collection.*

To get a taste of what it was like to be on deck when one of Foss's schooners was being loaded with "goatina," there is a rare book that was published in 1936 entitled *Last of the Five-Masters*. The author, Charles Merriam, luckily managed to talk Robert Rickson, skipper of Foss's schooner the *Edna Hoyt*, into allowing him to travel on the vessel. Not surprisingly, the *Edna Hoyt* was bound for Venezuela to load a cargo of goatina. We are lucky to have Merriam's description of this event—at least, until the procedure got so unbearable that Mr. Merriam decided to leave the *Hoyt* at the first opportunity. He began with a description of the first small sailboat that came alongside the schooner:

> *Making fast to us, her men started passing the sacks of manure over the side and across the deck to the after hatch where they were opened and their contents dumped into the hold. A stinking, blinding dust arose. Eyes smarted. Throats choked and pained. Only one hatch was being used. The prospect of what was to come when all the hatches were in use was not entrancing.*
>
> *The Mate shut the doors and windows of the cabin. Mr. Kelley* [the cook] *closed all the openings of the midshiphouse. But in spite of these*

The schooner *Harold G. Foss* (ex–*T.N. Barnsdall*), built in Camden, Maine, in 1920. Here she is pictured in Tampa Bay, Florida, being towed. *From the Foss Collection, courtesy of the Penobscot Marine Museum.*

Harold Foss's "other" five-master, the *Dunham Wheeler*, which was built in 1917 at the Percy & Small Shipyard in Bath, Maine. *From the Foss Collection, courtesy of the Penobscot Marine Museum.*

precautions a fine dust filtered into the living quarters and into the food. The sun rose and beat down mercilessly. The heat below was unbearable. I seized the opportunity afforded by the first boat unloaded and climbed aboard for a trip ashore.

The *Edna Hoyt* moored off Fort de France, Martinique. It must have been hot or rainy as a large canvas covers the aft part of the vessel. *From the Foss Collection, courtesy of the Penobscot Marine Museum.*

The Boston firm Foss & Crabtree operated six sailing vessels, which primarily worked the goatina trade and included the five-masters *Edna Hoyt* and *Dunham Wheeler* and the four-masters *Mabel*, *Edward L. Swan* (ex–*M. Vivian Peirce*), *General Leon Jurado* (ex–*Alice May Davenport*) and *Harold G. Foss* (ex–*T.N. Barnsdall*). It would seem that Captain Foss liked to rename vessels after people he knew! At one point, Foss also established the Superior Trading & Transportation Company.

After 1932, Foss shipped only a few cargoes per year. The four-masted schooner *Herbert L. Rawding*, a vessel that Foss rescued from the famous ship graveyard in Boothbay Harbor, Maine, carried the last cargo of goatina in 1941.

Due to the manufacture of fertilizer from synthetic sources and the increasing cost of labor, the guano business began to wane. The opening of the oil fields in Venezuela further added to the cost of labor. As the twentieth century marched on, the cost of maintaining sailing vessels and their eventual disappearance was something that even Captain Foss could not overcome.

TO FORESTALL THE END OF AN ERA

The Schooner Edna Hoyt

In December 1888, when the first five-masted schooner, *Governor Ames,* was launched in Waldoborough, Maine, the world was still very much enmeshed in the ways of the nineteenth century. In December 1920, however, when the last five-masted schooner, *Edna Hoyt*, was launched in Thomaston, Maine, she was quite clearly the last of her kind, an interloper in a mechanized, modern world. The fact that she was launched at all in 1920 is a miracle and a testament to Maine shipbuilders and mariners. The *Hoyt* was the fifty-sixth and final five-masted commercial schooner launched in the world.

According to official documents, the *Edna Hoyt* was launched on December 11, 1920, at the Dunn & Elliot Shipyard in Thomaston, Maine. She was 294.0 feet long, 41.1 feet wide and had a depth of 20.8 feet; her official number was 220938, and her signal letters were KNPS. Named after the wife of one of her original owners, the *Edna Hoyt* cost $280,000 to build back in 1920.

Built primarily for the coal trade, as were all of the large coasters, the *Edna Hoyt* would naturally take on any cargo she could between the coal runs. These cargoes became fewer and fewer as the decade drew to a close and steam colliers overtook sailing vessels. It also became increasingly difficult to obtain experienced crew members to sail her, a problem that plagued all commercial sailing vessels at the time. Designed to be operated by eleven

The first five-masted schooner, *Governor Ames*, loading lumber through her bow ports, circa 1890s. *Courtesy of the Somerset Historical Society.*

men, the five-masted *Edna Hoyt* often sailed with a crew of only nine. There was certainly a shortage of men who knew how to work a sailing vessel, and if given a choice, even experienced hands preferred to ship on steamers. With a steam-powered vessel you knew when you would arrive in port; on a sailing ship, there was never any guarantee as the vessel was dependent on the wind and weather. Living and working conditions were also much better aboard steamers and diesel-powered craft.

From her humble beginning as a collier she became a celebrity, and by the end of her career she was larger than life. In August 1934, when she lay at a wharf near Wall Street in New York City, her tall masts piercing the sky against the backdrop of towering skyscrapers, she was in many respects already a ghost. Because the enormous five-masted *Edna Hoyt* was the last of her kind, and everybody knew it, she caused quite a stir wherever she

The *Edna Hoyt* as she appeared on November 29, 1920, less than two weeks prior to launching. *Author's collection.*

went and could literally be followed in the headlines. The *Brooklyn Daily Eagle* carried this headline for August 1934: "City-Worn Youths Plead for Jobs on Last of 5-Masted Schooners." On September 30, 1934, the *Boston Herald* sported the following headline: "SURVIVOR! Her Days NUMBERED," and had this to tell its readers: "Five Masted Schooner *Edna Hoyt,* Last of Once Proud Fleet of Sailing Craft, Today Like Visitor from Mars When She Arrives in Port." On August 12, 1936, the *Daily Boston Globe* notified its readers, "Famous Schooner *Edna Hoyt* Expected." The *Quincy Patriot Ledger* reported on September 4, 1936, "World's Largest Schooner Is Here. Huge Sailing Ship Is the Last of Its Kind in Existence." The *Baltimore Sun,* on October 5, 1936, informed its readers that "the five-masted schooner *Edna*

The *Edna Hoyt* moments after launching at the Dunn & Elliot Shipyard in Thomaston, Maine. The note written in pencil on the back of this photo taken on December 11, 1920, reads, "Successfully launched." *Author's collection.*

Hoyt, one of the last of her kind, now is swinging at her mooring in the inner harbor."

Some adventures of the *Edna Hoyt* can be recounted briefly, and they were typical of events that commonly occurred on many coastal schooners. On December 23, 1928, a sailor who had broken his leg on the *Edna Hoyt* was taken aboard the steamship *San Benito* near Florida and brought to Long Wharf in Boston, the steamer's destination, where an ambulance was waiting. On January 16, 1929, the *Daily Boston Globe* reported:

> *More than two weeks overdue the schooner* Edna Hoyt *was towed into the harbor yesterday and tied up at McQuesten's Wharf, East Boston, where*

> *she will unload her cargo of 1,000,000 feet of hard pine. The vessel left Beaumont November 24.*

In October 1929, the *Hoyt* was more than a few weeks overdue while bringing a cargo from Venezuela to Boston, where she eventually discharged 2,200 tons of fertilizer at the Mystic Docks. Answering her distress signals, a steamer bound from Aruba to Boston sent a boat to the schooner to furnish the crew with provisions, as they had run out. Apparently, 1929 wasn't a very good year for the *Edna Hoyt*. The *Hoyt* was picked up near the Portland Lightship on December 10, 1929, as she was leaking, and towed to Searsport, Maine, by the coast guard cutter *Ossipee*. Assistance was requested when it was found that her cargo of fertilizer had plugged her bilges, making the pumps useless. On December 30, 1932, the *Edna Hoyt* was reported as being in distress, leaking at a rate of six inches an hour near the Diamond Shoals Lightship near Cape Hatteras, North Carolina. Thirty days out of Venezuela with a cargo of fertilizer she ran into heavy seas; the coast guard reported it had furnished three kegs of water to the men on the vessel, as the water supply was exhausted, and was sending a vessel to tow her into Norfolk, Virginia. The *Edna Hoyt* was taken in tow on July 20, 1935, by the coast guard cutter *Argot* when her rudder became twisted near Martha's Vineyard. The *Hoyt*'s master, Robert Rickson, was traveling with his wife and daughter, who both went ashore. In 1936, there must have been a lot of people in Boston who misbehaved, as the *Edna Hoyt* is reported to have delivered 2,500 tons of coal to that port on Christmas Day. These are just a few of the many reports of this vessel that are listed in newspaper archives and contained in yellowed folders in numerous places.

The *Edna Hoyt* carried various cargoes throughout her lengthy career, including lumber, coal, phosphate rock, fertilizer, salt, automobiles, barbed wire, building supplies and silk stockings. When the *Hoyt* left New York City in August 1934, she was carrying two dozen pairs of the finest silk stockings that money could buy. It would seem that owner Harold Foss ordered these for his business partner, Leon Jurardo, president of the state of Falcon, Venezuela. This unusual bit of information was reported by the *Daily Boston Globe* on August 25, 1934.

The phenomenon of the *Edna Hoyt* as a celebrity may be similar to that of the famed racehorse Seabiscuit, both heroes of the 1930s. In a Depression-worn era, people were starving for heroes, for a distraction, for some means of escape. An escape into the past, to the much-romanticized age of sail, must have seemed quite enticing to most folks.

Moored at the foot of Wall Street in New York City, her five elegant masts piercing the sky against the backdrop of looming skyscrapers, the schooner *Edna Hoyt* appeared ghost-like. It was August 1934, and by now she *was* a ghost. Lying at the wharf, lingering amidst automobiles and seaplanes, the *Edna Hoyt* drew an estimated crowd of over fifty thousand sightseers while she was in New York City. Over five hundred young men demanded to be taken aboard as sailors, willing to work without pay. They wanted to escape the city and live a dream, or what they thought would be a dream.

There were so many enthusiastic visitors to the vessel that they even broke the gangplank. Owner Harold Foss had to come from Maine to help

The *Edna Hoyt* tied up at the foot of Wall Street in New York City, August 1934. *Courtesy of the Maine Maritime Museum.*

control the crowds and to speak to reporters! Some of the most notable people on Wall Street came to visit the *Edna Hoyt*. Kermit Roosevelt, son of late president Theodore Roosevelt, was among those who visited the ship. Dr. Herman Baruch, U.S. ambassador and brother to financier and political consultant Bernard Baruch, visited the schooner every morning and afternoon.

Another event quite worthy of note occurred in November 1935 in Portland, Maine. In contrast to the five hundred young men who demanded jobs on the *Hoyt* when she was tied up in New York City the summer before, when the large schooner was moored in Portland Harbor, Captain Rickson could find no crew to sail her. Witnesses say that the *Hoyt*, deeply laden with her cargo, rode restlessly at anchor in Portland, tugging at her moorings as if she wanted to leave with the tide. Portland is significantly different than New York City in many ways, especially in gray November, when more than a hint of the forbidding winter season is stirring in the air. The sailors in Portland *were* sailors and knew of the hardships involved in working a sailing vessel. Most preferred to steer clear of that sort of work.

"The sailors around here don't want to work," Captain Rickson told *Christian Science Monitor* reporter Harlen Trott in an interview on November 14.

"A man's got to sleep," a local sailor explained in the same interview. "And precious little you'll ever get in a shorthanded hooker like her."

"Imagine shifting topsails in a wind wagon like that every time they tacked ship?" another old salt added. "With chain sheets so heavy that they'd all but pull a fellow off the doublings."

Mrs. Rickson, who was aboard the schooner at the time of the interview, told reporters that she liked sailing with her husband "in a calm," but when a breeze came up, she preferred to remain on land.

After Captain Rickson paced back and forth and "whistled" for a wind, the *Edna Hoyt* eventually got underway on November 23, carrying seven thousand bundles of barrel shooks destined for a port in Barbados. Rickson had to send to Norfolk, Virginia, for a cook and sailed the big schooner with a crew of eight instead of the eleven that would have been ideal.

Author Charles Merriam describes his first glimpse of the *Edna Hoyt* when she was tied up in Portland in 1935 in the following excerpt from his book *Last of the Five-Masters*:

> *In these days of steam and calculated speed large sailing ships are a rare sight. Therefore there was something stirring in the picture; something pulse-quickening; something that loomed against the backdrop of Portland's venerable waterfront like an illustrated page of American History.*

Merriam eventually persuaded Captain Rickson to allow him to sail on the large schooner and agreed to meet the vessel in Norfolk, Virginia, and from there sail with the crew to South America. Merriam described his first visit to the schooner in Portland:

> *The decks had been recently scoured. The paint was scrubbed bright; the gear neatly coiled; the great sails smoothly furled and covered. A United States shield adorned the base of the spankermast, brilliant with new paint.*

For two weeks, the *Hoyt* was anchored off the Virginia coast as the captain and crew waited for a breeze and fair weather. One evening, Merriam wrote, "night fell with an unusually thick fog. Ghostly halos glowed about the mooring lanterns."

Eventually they got underway, but not long afterward a raging storm threatened to destroy the large schooner. Merriam wrote:

> *The ship shook from keel to masthead. A dreadful force seemed to be wrenching at her vitals. I jumped up the companionway and looked through a light port. The afterdeck was entirely covered. The men at the helm, up to their necks in seething water, clung to the wheel for their lives.*

When the heavy hawser line was thrown over the stern to try to stabilize the ship and didn't work, the captain ordered that lubricating oil be thrown overboard to serve the same purpose. Again, it was to no avail. Nothing would settle the wild, angry seas. When the boatswain reported there was a foot of water in the bilge, the engineer started the pumps. The heavy seas tossed the large vessel as if she were a toy. After another particularly thunderous crash, Merriam recounted:

> *The rail, a solid piece of oak twelve by four inches thick had been snapped in two. An iron brace had been torn from the deck and had broken a plank three inches thick. Our only lifeboat had been smashed.*

A tall, well-dressed Harold Foss shakes hands with Robert Rickson, who was master of the *Edna Hoyt* in 1934. *Harold Foss.*

This is not a work of fiction; rather, it is an eyewitness account of a voyage on a five-masted schooner in the mid-1930s. Fortunately, the *Edna Hoyt* survived this ordeal, along with her crew members. Even seasoned mariner Robert Rickson, concerned that his ship might succumb to the weather, had the following advice for his passenger:

> *It won't take long if she starts to break up. She can't stand this pounding much longer. Nothing I know of could. There's nothing that you can do. Just step over the side and get it over with as quickly and as painlessly as possible. It's happened to thousands and it will happen to thousands more.*

The *Hoyt* miraculously managed to escape this gale, and author Charles Merriam went on to write more books. Captain Rickson took over the schooner *Herbert Rawding*, and a new master for the *Edna Hoyt* emerged: Captain George Hopkins.

The *Edna Hoyt* entered Boston Harbor on September 12, 1937, with 1,650 tons of salt from Turks Island, after a seventeen-day trip.

"It was only a fair run for the *Hoyt*," Captain George Hopkins stated during an interview with a Boston reporter. "But for the fact that we were becalmed for five days off Nantucket Lightship we would have covered the distance in twelve days," he added.

Unfortunately, in just over one month on October 14, 1937, the elegant five-master would embark on a journey from which she would never return. Captain Hopkins had no way of knowing, as nobody does, that the end was about to come and that time would catch up with his celebrated wind-driven craft.

The *Edna Hoyt* was representative of an era that had nearly passed out of existence by the time her stern hit the St. George River in Thomaston, Maine, on the day of her launching. She will always be associated with Captain Harold Foss, the man who forestalled the end of an era, at least for a little while Down East.

Of his beloved five-sticker, Captain Harold Foss was quoted by journalist Fred Hunt in the September 4, 1936 edition of the *Quincy Patriot Ledger* as saying, "The *Edna Hoyt* is the last of her line. When she goes, there will be none left."

THE LAST LOG OF THE *EDNA HOYT*

It really is a miracle that she made it as far as she did. The loss of the *Edna Hoyt*, that elegant sailing vessel that carried many thousands of yards of sail and no engine at all to propel her, certainly signaled the end of the big coasters. There may have been a few four-masters left in service, and maybe some three-masters, but the end would come soon, and men like owner Harold Foss knew it, although he likely didn't speak of it.

The last voyage of the *Edna Hoyt* began with a routine stop at a coal pier in southern Wales, at Newport. She was to pick up a load of coal to take to Venezuela, and then she would return to the States loaded with goatina to discharge at a fertilizer plant in New England.

The five-masted schooner was about to embark on her last voyage, a journey into oblivion, and we will experience the events of that tragic excursion through the eyes and ears of one of the men who sailed her. Her master on this trip was Captain George Hopkins, an experienced skipper who often brought his wife out to sea with him. Luckily, she wasn't with him this time.

In a research room at the Penobscot Marine Museum in Searsport, Maine, surrounded by oil paintings depicting sailing vessels that have long since passed into the realm of the forgotten, I was handed the logbook of the *Edna Hoyt* by museum volunteer Don Garrold.

"We are glad we were able to find that for you," museum collections manager Cipperly Good stated, smiling.

On the front cover of the stained, nondescript ledger book, I saw the name *Edna Hoyt* handwritten with what appeared to be a fountain pen, and beneath that somebody had added the words "Log & Final Papers." Unfortunately, history has not shared the name of the log writer. Usually, it was the first or second mate who kept the log, but not always so. About one-quarter through the log, the first entry appears, after the heading "Log of the Schr. *Edna Hoyt*." To one who is familiar with the story of the schooner *Edna Hoyt* and her inevitable demise, the first few entries in her last logbook seem to prophesize doom. The *Hoyt* was a very large wooden vessel. Her official specifications were listed as follows: tonnage, 1,512 pounds; overall length, 294.0 feet; breadth, 41.1 feet; and depth 20.8 feet. A vessel nearly 300 feet long with the breadth and depth of the *Hoyt* required an ample berth at the dock.

> *Thursday the 14th day of Oct. 1937*
> *This Noon Anchored off Newport Roads. 1 pm took tow boat and pilot and proceeded on up to the Arrow Fewell* [fuel] *Co. Dock on the Newport River. Took boat to assist towboat to Dock schr. 430 pm tied up to the wharf. Vessil ebbed Dry on Low water.*
> *So ends the day.*
>
> *Friday the 15th Day of Oct. 1937*
> *Abt 10AM this day started to load cargo* [coal] *vessil hard aground, but put about 400 tons of fewel* [coal]. *This day at Low Water vessil high and dry and not resting well, pressing hard against wharf on two spilings one shoud of main riging carried away. So ends the Day.*
>
> *Saturday the 16th Day of Oct. 1937*
> *At 7 am started work on cargo, at 10 am Master and Boatswain went down under vessils bottom and found the Bottom Hard and vessil resting only on keel Bottom and Bildge free seven but seemed to be strained. Master ordered work stopped and protested against Berth not being safe, arranged for survey for the night, Low tide at 11 pm. One surveyar for the shipper one for ship. The broker, the Master and Boatswain went under the Bottom and examined the vessil and Berth. So ends the day.*

Sunday the 17th Day of Oct. 1937
At 4 am Pilot and two tow Boats came and Took Vessil from Dock by orders of Master, proceeded down to Newport Roads about 7 miles away to a Place where Vessil could Lay afloat, strong tide running. Set sea watches and kept one man at the wheel at all times.

The unfortunate events of the first few days at the Welsh coal pier certainly seemed to bode disaster for the large schooner. The side of the ship was damaged, and part of the rigging that supports the mast was torn away. The *Hoyt* lay at anchor near Newport Roads until October 28, when arrangements were made to finish loading her with coal in Cardiff. On the same day, the schooner was towed to the Crown Fuel Wharf in Cardiff, Wales, to complete the loading. We return to the log on the next day:

Friday the 29th day of Oct. 1937
Worked on cargo this day untill 4:30 and finished loading 1755 tons in all. Draft forward 21.11, aft 22.07. Hauled vessil away from the Dock to make room for another ship. So ends the day.

Saturday the 30th Day of Oct. 1937
This day crew employed making vessil ready for sea. So ends the day.

Sunday the 31st Day of Oct. 1937
Doing no work of any kind this Day. Vessil now Laying outside of a Russian SS. So ends the day.

Monday the 1st Day of Nov. 1937
This day Master clearing ship and crew making ready for sea and taking stores on board. So ends the day.

Tuesday the 2nd Day of Nov. 1937
At 4 am Tow Boat and pilot came and took vessil and proceeded out of dock. Picked up outside tug and pilot and proceeded to sea. At 10:30 am Tow Boat let vessil go. Off Nash Point set all sail. Wind Light Easterly. 4 hrs almost calm. 8 hrs light airs from the East. So ends the day.

Wednesday the 3rd Day of Nov. 1937
This Day comes in with overcast and moderate weather. 4 hrs passed Lindy Island, wind Light weather cloudy. All sail set. Day ends without change.

Thursday the 4th Day of Nov. 1937
This day came in with fresh southerly wind and Rough seas. 8 am took in all Light Sails. Noon Lat 50°56'00" long. 8°17'00". 4 pm Blowing hard with nasty Rough sea. Reefed spanker, took in flying jib. 8 pm strong wind heavy sea, vessil labouring Heavy. Took in foresail and Jiger sail. Vessil making much extra water. Day ends without change.

The large schooners were originally equipped with steam and later gasoline- and diesel-powered "donkey" engines, which were used for raising the sails, raising the anchor and also pumping water out of the hold. It was common for some water to seep in through the wooden hulls on these overworked and often overloaded wooden vessels, but the notation in the log that the "vessil [was] making much extra water" is certainly ominous and likely a result of the damage done at the dock in Newport, as well as the age of the ship.

It becomes clear to the reader of these ships' logs that spelling wasn't a prerequisite for being hired on as a seaman on a sailing vessel. The phrase "took in foresail and Jiger sail" refers to the names of the masts on a five-masted schooner, from which the names of the sails are derived. On a five-masted schooner, the masts are named as such: fore, main, mizzen, spanker and jigger. The jigger is the last or fifth mast, and the fore is the first. The jibs are the smaller triangular sails that are set forward of the foremast on the bowsprit or jib boom. To "reef" a sail means to reduce the sail area; on a schooner, it would mean to partly lower the sail.

Friday, the 5th Day of Nov. 1937
This day comes in with nasty weather. Very heavy sea and heavy Gale from the South. 8 am took in mizen sail, vessil making heavy weather. Noon by DR Lat 50°50'00 Long 9°30'00. 4 pm wind backing to N & E strong. 8 pm wind moderating, set lower sail. Day ends with strong ENE wind, vessil making much extra water. Pumps carefully atd.

The notation "pumps carefully atd" means that the pumps that were pumping excess water out of the hold were carefully attended to, a very serious matter on a wooden sailing vessel loaded with 2,155 tons of coal and "making much extra water."

> *Saturday the 6th Day of Nov. 1937*
> *This day comes in with strong ENE winds and cloudy weather. Sailing with 4 Big sails and Reefed Spanker with 2 Head sails. Noon Lat by DD 40°53'00 Long 10°40'00. 4 pm strong Breeze Rough sea with cloudy weather. Vessil still making Lots of water. Pumps carefully atd. This day ends with weather moderating and sea running down.*
>
> *Sunday the 7th Day of Nov. 1937*
> *This day comes in with moderate wind and partly clear weather with moderate sea, all sail set. Noon Lat by Abs. 47°29'00" Long 13°46'00". 4 pm no change in weather, 8 pm Overcast fresh breeze SE, took in all Light sail with reefed spanker. Vessil still making extra water. So ends the day.*
>
> *Monday the 8th Day of Nov. 1937*
> *This day comes in with fresh breeze and very heavy swell from the SSE, Noon Lat. By Abs. 45°29'00 Long 14°27'40". 4 pm fresh breeze with very heavy SSE swell & Rough sea, Vessil making much water, pumps carefully atd. So ends the Day.*
>
> *Tuesday the 9th Day of Nov. 1937*
> *This day comes in with nasty weather, strong SE wind with rough sea. Noon Reefed vessil down, took in flying jib. Lat, by D.R. 42°29'00" Long. 17°40'00". Vessil making much water, about twice the usual amount, pumps carefully atd. Day ends overcast with strong wind and very rough sea.*
>
> *Wednesday, the 10th Day of Nov. 1937*
> *This day comes in with strong wind and Heavy seas. Vessil making good headway but labouring Hard. Noon Lat, by D.R. 40°00' 00" Long. 18°30' 00". Wind backing to the Eastward, 4 pm Blowing Heavy wind East with Very High and Rough seas. Pumps carefully atd. So ends this day.*

Thursday the 11th Day of Nov. 1937
This day comes in with Heavy Gale from the Eastward with rough sea and very Heavy southerly swell. Noon Lat. 39°30'00" Long 20°00'00". 4 pm Heavy Gale SSE with very High and rough sea. All headsail in and vessil laying Hove to on PT, Vessil making almost as much water as pumps can take care of, pumps carefully atd. So ends the day.

While reading this log, one wonders just how much punishment a wooden vessel can take and remain serviceable. With so many consecutive days of fierce punishment, it is certainly a testament to her builders that the *Edna Hoyt* could remain afloat. With the vessel laboring hard and leaking so badly that the pumps could barely keep up, disaster was certainly imminent unless the weather changed for the better quickly. (A vessel that is "hove to" is riding out the storm where she takes the seas most comfortably rather than trying to make progress.)

Friday the 12th Day of Nov. 1937
This day comes in with Heavy SSE Gale and an awful high sea. Vessil still Hove to and making about as much water as pumps can handle. Noon by D.R. Lat 40°30' Long 20°10' 00". Examined vessil under Decks and found several of the Between Deck Beams Broken and cargo from Between Deck Dropped, especially in Hatches. Day ends without change.

Saturday the 13th Day of Nov. 1937
This day comes in without change. Vessil Hove to, but making bad weather. 8 am Wind Hawling to the South, put Head sail up and spanker down, wore ship around to star tack, Noon making better weather and not labouring quite so hard. Noon by D.R. Lat 41°00' 00" Long 20°00' 00". 6 pm put one sailor in Engine Room to help out with pump, have to keep pumps going near all the time. Vessil working and labouring hard again. So Ends the Day.

Sunday the 14th day of Nov. 1937
This day comes in with Heavy Gale from the south, with Heavy seas. Vessil washing and labouring hard. Abt noon vessil labouring so hard and washing so bad we had to run vessil off before the wind. Position about Lat 41°30' 00" Long 19°40' 00". Vessil running under reefed fore sail,

shipping Heavy seas. 8 pm no change in weather, Vessil making all the water pumps can take care of. So Ends the Day.

Monday the 15th Day of Nov. 1937
No change in weather. Worse if any change. 4 am wind shifted to SW full Gale, with awful seas. Vessil running well, but shipping tons of water. Noon heavy rain squalls and gusts of wind. Pumps going most all the time. Day ends without change.

Tuesday the 16th Day of Nov. 1937
This day comes in with wind moderating and sea somewhat less. Vessil still running before the wind, Noon Lat 41°33'00" Long 17°39'00". 4 pm Nasty weather, rain squalls with Heavy wind and awful heavy seas. 8 pm No change in weather. So Ends the Day. Pumps carefully atd.

At this point in the log, it sounds pretty ominous, and the twenty-first-century reader already knows the end of the story. The fact that the decks below have collapsed has already ushered in the death knell for this once-sturdy sailing vessel. Even if she made it to her destination in Venezuela, the extensive repairs required to put her back into good condition would be too costly to consider.

Wednesday the 17th Day of Nov. 1937
This day comes in with wind moderating. This am made Life Boat Ready in case we had to Leave vessil. 10 am wind and sea moderate enough to let the vessil come by the wind. Wind about WNW Lat. Noon 42°42 Long 14°19'. Master decided to run for Lisbon Portugal. 8 pm weather overcast and squally. So Ends the Day.

Thursday the 18th Day of Nov. 1937
Thursday comes in with squally weather and moderate winds Southerly to SE. Heavy swell from West N West. Noon Lat. 43°00'00" Long 13°30'. We're not making quite so much water. Pumps carefully atd. So ends the day.

Friday the 19th Day of Nov. 1937
This day comes in with moderate and squally weather with Heavy westerly swell. Noon Lat. 40°00' Long 11°30'00". 4 pm Light northerly wind

with rain squalls. Heavy swells. 8 pm No change in weather, Pumps carefully atd. So ends the Day.

Saturday the 20th Day of Nov. 1937
This day comes in with moderate variable winds, mostly north East to North. Noon Lat. 40°30' Long 11°11'00". 4 pm Squally shifting winds with very Heavy Northerly swell. 8 pm Moderate wind from the NNE. Pumps carefully atd.

Sunday the 21st Day of Nov. 1937
This day comes in with clear weather and moderate wind from the N., with moderate Northerly swell. At 2 am made Light on Burling Island. Noon Burling Island Light abeam. Bearing NE½E set all lower sail. Wind Light, weather clear. 4 pm Wind hawled back to SSW and Heavy swell from the NW. Tacked off shore. Day ends with squally weather and moderate wind, pumps well atd.

Monday the 22nd Day of Nov. 1937
This day comes in with moderate westerly wind. 1 am Tacked ship and headed to the southard. Heavy swell from the NW. Noon Cape Roca Bearing SSE 15 miles, wind moderate and hawling back to the southard, strong current setting to the North. 4 pm vessil close in under Cape Roca. Heavy swell setting in from the westward, wind about SSW. Tacked ship and stood off shore again. This Day ends squally with heavy rain. Pumps well atd. Vessil still making much water.

This log likely hasn't seen the light of day for a half century or more. Today, the reader can absorb all the events leading up to the end of this magnificent vessel and do so in a relaxed manner. There aren't any howling winds or torrential rains descending on us as we read from this logbook, long since covered with dust and written by a sailor who has already passed into another realm. I wonder if today we can fully appreciate words like "nasty weather, awful heavy seas, vessil labouring hard." The *Edna Hoyt* didn't even have a radio in 1937, although every steamship was equipped with one. The crew and captain on this five-masted schooner were completely alone out on the sea, at the mercy of the elements. Can we even imagine what it was like to be on a sailing vessel with heavy seas continuously washing over the decks, water seeping through the weakened wooden hull as fast as it could be pumped out, heavy rains and winds and high seas? It would be difficult to sit in the galley to eat, with plates and cups sliding every which way, and even more troublesome for the cook to prepare the meals. As far as getting a good night's rest, the exhausted, wet sailor would constantly be tossed and turned in his narrow bunk, water dripping in from above deck. The list of legitimate complaints would likely be endless by today's standards.

The references to "tacking" the ship mean changing direction by shifting the sails, usually back and forth in a zigzag pattern, with the bow heading into the wind. This method of maneuvering a sailing vessel against the wind required lots of work and lots of room on the ocean. The *Edna Hoyt* was a five-masted schooner with a crew of only eleven men. The log entry for Monday, November 22, "1 am Tacked ship," certainly indicates that these sailors were working around the clock under adverse weather conditions. It is no wonder it was so difficult to find qualified crew members to work on such vessels.

If this log had been written in the eighteenth or nineteenth centuries, it would not be remarkable. Sailing vessels were tossed and torn apart on the ocean quite often in earlier centuries, but the *Edna Hoyt* was a twentieth-century vessel, and this was 1937. Even Mother Nature seemed to know that it was the end of the "Age of Sail" and that this large five-masted vessel was an aberration. The ways of nature often seem unkind, and perhaps that is why it punished the vessel so. All logic seemed to indicate that this wooden-hulled, wind-driven ship should finally succumb. The damage at the Newport, Wales coal dock combined with the continued bouts of incessant foul weather certainly put the nails in the coffin for this old girl. Insurmountable difficulties persisted as the log continued:

> *Wednesday the 24th Day of Nov. 1937*
> *Squally. 4 pm Cape Roca Bearing about E X S 3 miles. Mainsail carried away. Heavy swell with very light wind from the SSW. Wore ship and let vessil head off shore. Vessil just about holding own. 4:45 pm put up distress signals and spoke Norwegian ship* San Miguel, *asked for assistance. Master of SS ship agreed to take vessil in tow. 5:20 pm put schooner's boat out and ran line to steam ship, got line to ship and hove ships line to schr. Steam ship backed some distance off with vessil in order to have room to drift while getting towing hawser to schr. Cape Roca Light Bearing about E X S two miles and half. About 8:30 pm have towing*

hawser fast to schr. Proceeded on toward Lisbon. Weather squally with heavy rain and fresh SSE wind. So ends the Day. Pumps well atd. and water well under control.

Thursday the 25th Day of Nov. 1937
This day comes in with Heavy rain and nasty weather. Fresh SE wind at 6:30 am. Came to anchor in Lisbon Harbor at noon. Finished San Miguel. Tried to moor at another anchorage with tug Cabo Especial *but current was too strong to get anchor. 3 pm tow boat and pilot came again and moved vessel to another anchorage. Let out 75 fathoms of chain. Vessil not making so much water as when outside. Pumps carefully atd. So Ends the Day.*

Friday the 26th Day of Nov. 1937
This day Master went on shore to enter, etc. Also to Consul entered protest etc. Day ends without anything of importance.

Saturday the 27th Day of Nov. 1937
This day survey held on vessil by two different parties, one by ship and one by port officials. Recommend Discharging cargo complete, all Between Deck Beams found to be broken on port side. Deck and cargo saged Down to cargo in lower hold, also some beams on star. side broken, stern of vessil twisted. Vessil not making so much water at the Time about 45 minutes pumping with wrecking pump every 4 hours. So Ends the Day.

Sunday the 28th Day of Nov. 1937
This day doing no work of any kind this day.

Inserted in the back of the logbook I found a separate document, written by Captain Hopkins himself. It was a customary statement explaining his decision to head to Lisbon, Portugal, where he asked a passing steamer to tow his vessel into that port:

The reason that assistance was asked of SS San Miguel *was that with the wind SSE and the vessel leaking badly, I the Master, was afraid that the vessel would not stand another gale, and in duty to myself, crew, ship, and*

cargo, in my opinion thought it necessary to have the vessel towed to Lisbon.
Geo. A. Hopkins, Master

So ends the last log of the last five-masted commercial sailing vessel. Owner Harold Foss reluctantly ordered her sold to pay salvage claims. What was left of the *Edna Hoyt* was purchased by the Portuguese and used as a floating coal barge, reduced to being drawn at the end of a towline. Nevermore would her long masts pierce the endless skies or her expansive, majestic bowsprit point the way to far-off lands.

The majestic bowsprit of the *Edna Hoyt* proudly displayed against the backdrop of skyscrapers at the foot of Wall Street in August 1934. *Harold Foss.*

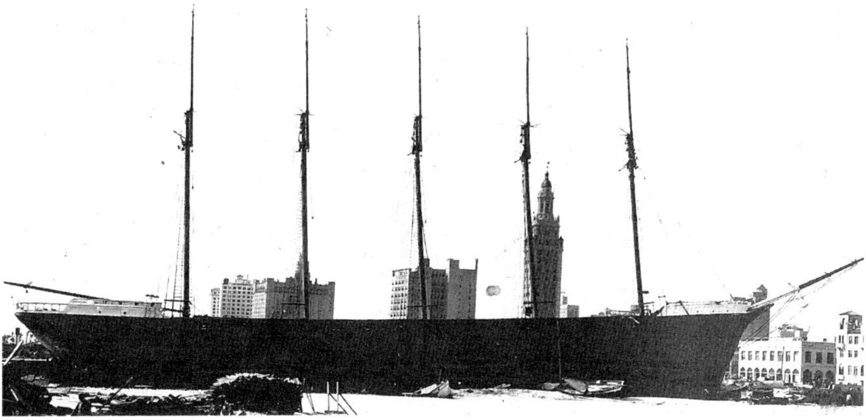

A five-masted schooner washed ashore after a storm in Miami, 1926. *Author's collection.*

After returning to the States on the American steamer *Excello*, Captain George Hopkins turned over the *Hoyt*'s papers, logbook and chronometer to owner Captain Harold Foss. Afterward, Hopkins was offered commands on many steamships, to which he is reputed to have replied, according to a 1964 article in *Down East* magazine, "Thank you, no. I'm going to be faithful to the *Edna Hoyt.* The time has come for me to go on the beach. Since there are no more sailing vessels in want of a master, I'd rather be on the beach than take command of a steamer."

Epilogue

THE AFTERMATH

In the wake of all this history and the great age of sail, what have we left today? Unfortunately, the big schooners are gone. The four-masted *Margaret Todd* is a steel-hulled replica, and the *Victory Chimes* is the only working three-masted schooner left. The *Victory Chimes*, a Delaware schooner, was brought to Maine in 1954 by Captain Fredrick Guild, who was first inspired to own his own schooner after sailing on the *Edna Hoyt* in the 1930s. Alas, Captain Harold Foss still influences what we see on the Maine coast today. He believed his commitment to the sea was in his blood.

"It is only natural that one should be interested in, and desirous of, knowing about his ancestors and their origin. As years pass by, this interest deepens." These are the opening sentences in Harold Foss's unpublished history of his own family. On the following page, Foss proudly chronicles the life of John Foss, whom he tells his reader first came to Boston Harbor about 1660 in an English navy vessel. Believing he would like to remain in the New World, the young sailor jumped ship and ended up in Portsmouth, New Hampshire. The family eventually came to Down East Maine.

On the schooner *Lewis R. French*, Captain Garth Wells had to say of the Fosses, "The name Foss is very well known here along the coast. There's even a Foss out here today."

A three-masted or "tern" schooner somewhere in the Penobscot Bay Region. This photo was taken about 1918. *Author's collection.*

"Would that be Captain John Foss of the schooner *American Eagle*?" I asked. I recalled that during my research I found much information online about the windjammer *American Eagle*.

"Yes, he's right out here in the bay with us today. Would you like me to raise him on the radio?" Captain Wells inquired.

Captain Wells did find Captain Foss on his ship's radio. Captain John Foss recalled Harold Foss and knew of the role he played in shipping in the early twentieth century.

Another who recalled Harold Foss was his nephew Robert (Bob). It would seem that Captain Harold Foss, not unlike others in his vocation, had a propensity for spinning yarns. The following discussion with Bob is testimony.

"He used to tell good stories," Bob Foss explained.

> *Actually, I'm a little embarrassed that I believed most of them when I was a kid.*
>
> *When I was twelve, I remember Uncle Harold showing me a huge snakeskin, so big that it went most of the length of the wall in his barn. Well, you know that he traveled all over the world, and he had the opportunity to find things like this. He told me that the snake tried to attack him. He said it slithered right up to him, opened its large jaws and just as it was about to strike, he pulled out his silver revolver and shot it in the nick of time. Then he took me by the shoulder, walked me to the back of the barn and pointed to the snake's tail. "See that hole?" he asked. "That's where the bullet came out."*

Ralph Stanley from Southeast Harbor on Mount Desert remembered Harold Foss as well. "I certainly knew of him, he was pretty famous around here," he said. "But I didn't know him personally."

We were seated in the Stanleys' front parlor talking about schooners and stories of shipwrecks when I mentioned that I would have a few chapters about the town of Hancock in the book.

"I was born in Hancock," Marion Stanley declared. "When my parents were up in Hancock, they were doing lobstering," she added. "And my grandfather worked in the roundhouse at the Mount Desert Ferry. My grandparents had a farm in Hancock, near the Carrying Place."

In the galley of the schooner *French*, with the vessel pitching in a summer rainsquall, I held onto my mug so that it wouldn't slide across the table.

Scott, the cook, hailed from Mount Desert. "I'm from Bar Harbor," he said. "Did you know that Bar Harbor used to be known as the town of Eden?"

"No, I didn't know. That's very interesting," I said, dodging drops of water that were coming in from above deck. "Are you familiar with the town of Hancock?"

"Of course. My father built lobster boats, and we used to go to Hancock Point all the time for lobsters," he said, picking up a potholder so that he could open the door of the wood stove. "That's hot," he said, putting a few more pieces of oak into the chamber. "What makes you want to write about the island?"

"I have some ancestors who were among the first to settle there, the Richardsons and the Gotts," I answered, wiping a droplet of either rainwater or perspiration from my forehead. Although it was August, the only way to cook food aboard the schooner was to keep the wood stove going all day. It must have been over ninety degrees in the small ship's galley.

"My grandmother was a Gott!" Scott declared, smiling. "Hello, cousin."

I had no idea when I left my home in Massachusetts to return to Maine for a sail on a nineteenth-century schooner that I would find so many blood ties.

Maine maritime history has left its traces in Massachusetts, too. Many older Boston residents have fond memories of Maine ships. Bill Danner, a ninety-two-year-old former resident of East Boston, still remembers the days when the large Maine schooners would tie up at the wharf.

"So you remember the big Down East coasters?" I asked.

"Of course," Bill answered. "I used to see them often at McQuesten's Wharf, in East Boston." He paused and then added, "And then I saw them laid up at the Meridian Street Bridge."

"What details do you remember?" I asked. "And what were the names of the schooners you saw?"

Bill chuckled at my naiveté. "McQuesten's was a working wharf. The schooners just tied up and discharged their cargo. They didn't stay around for long; time was money. And I didn't take notes."

Bill remembered large schooners like the five-masted *Jennie Flood Krieger* (the largest ship built in Belfast, Maine, in 1919), lying idle at the Meridian Street Bridge.

"I boarded her lots of times. We'd swing on the lines and dive off her side," he explained. "Later, after a few kids were hurt on the ships, they moved them away."

As he spoke of the schooners, he paused, smiled and closed his eyes. I knew he had gone back to visit them at that wharf in East Boston once again—so, too, will we someday pause to recall.

There are no rock-strewn coastlines or crashing waves washing up along the shore of the southeastern Massachusetts town in which I live, nearly forty miles from the ocean. That's why it is so unbelievable that I found the granddaughter of Captain Almus Foss, the master of the schooner *W.H. Card* mentioned in a previous chapter, living only three miles from my home.

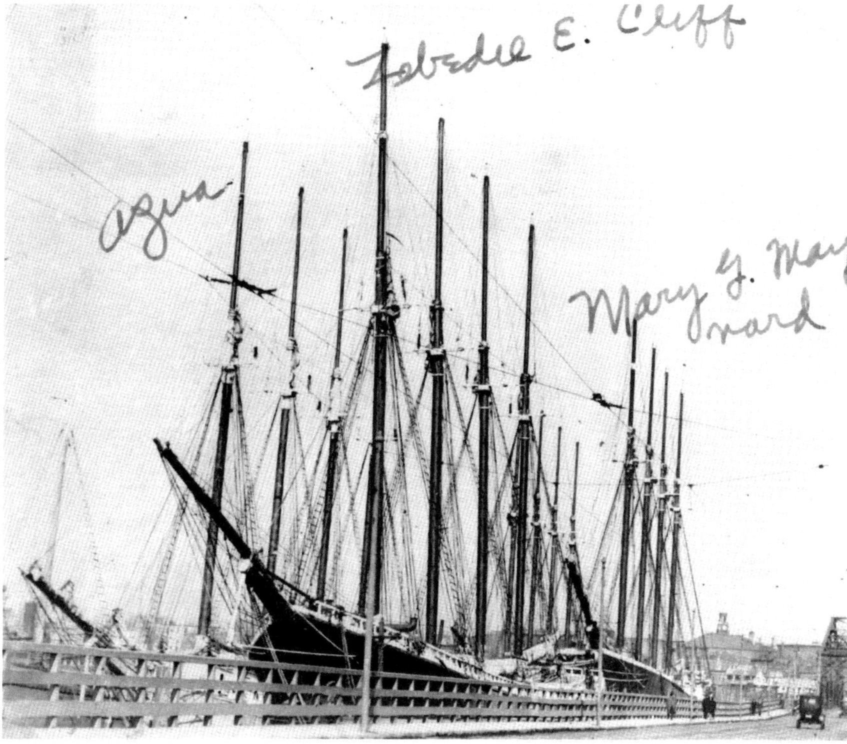

Maine schooners at the Meridian Street Bridge in East Boston. *From the Foss Collection, courtesy of the Penobscot Marine Museum.*

When I visited Clara Foss Johnston, she had recently celebrated her ninety-third birthday. Not surprisingly, her home was full of antiques and maritime artifacts.

"I wasn't born in Hancock, I was born here," she explained. "My father's people were from Maine. They lived by the sea in and around Hancock."

Although Clara stood stooped over a cane, her eyes were bright and piercing.

"We would go back there in the summertime like some wild thing returning to its birthplace," she said, a smile lighting up her face. "This was back in the '20s. We seemed to be irresistibly drawn to the salt water as if it were a kind of magnet. The Atlantic was in the blood of all of our people."

"You come from a family of seafarers?" I asked.

"My great-grandfather's ships sailed up and down the coast with cargoes of lumber, and my grandfather followed him in this trade." Clara paused, smiled and then added, "The great Atlantic fed us all in one way or another."

Just after the end of the First World War, these youthful members of the "lost generation" recline along the edge of the Penobscot River surveying a Maine schooner that has sailed into history. *Author's collection.*

History will come alive anywhere, if you know where to look. Is there anything the twenty-first-century explorer can rediscover along the coast of Maine? A few places still remain where we can enjoy, if only for a brief moment, the long-forgotten flavor of another era. Maine maritime history is still alive. It lives in the blood of the descendants and in the vessels that still work the coast.

Perhaps Norumbega can really be found in Down East Maine after all. The problem has been that for centuries those who have tried to find it were looking for gold, silver and pearls. Wealth can be measured in many ways, however, and the riches that one can discover along the coast of Maine are far more valuable than precious metals. In Maine, Down East and otherwise, in the Penobscot Bay region and in Hancock County, history will come alive again for the perceptive observer. The sights and sounds of another era are lying in wait for those who wish to tarry amongst them. In this fast-paced, computer-generated world, perhaps we should all get out to sea on a Maine schooner, let the crisp ocean breeze tousle our hair and sail into another century. Perhaps this could be the greatest treasure of all.

BIBLIOGRAPHY

Adams, James Truslow. *The Founding of New England.* Boston: Atlantic Monthly Press, 1921.

Arber, Edward. *An English Garner.* Vol. 2. Birmingham, UK: Arber, 1879.

Baltimore Sun. "Light Winds Force Schooner to Take Month for Voyage." October 5, 1936.

Barry, John Stetson. *History of Massachusetts, First Period.* Boston: Phillips, Sampson and Company, 1855.

Bernard, Sir Francis. "Journal of a Voyage to the Island of Mount Desart, 1762." *Bangor Historical Magazine* (April 1887).

Bishop, Leander J. *A History of American Manufacturers from 1608 to 1860.* Vol. 1. Philadelphia: S.A. George, 1861.

Boston Herald. "Survivor! Her Days Numbered." September 30, 1934.

Boston Port Authority and Writers of the WPA. *Boston Looks Seaward: The Story of the Port, 1630 to 1940.* Boston: Bruce Humphries Incorporated, 1941.

Bowker, Frank. *Atlantic Four-Master: The Story of the* Herbert L. Rawding. Mystic, CT: Mystic Seaport Museum, 1986.

———. *Blue Water Coaster.* Camden, ME: International Marine Publishing Company, 1972.

———. *Hull-Down.* New Bedford, MA: Reynolds-DeWalt, 1963.

Bryant, William Cullen, and Sydney Howard Gay. *Bryant's History of the United States*. Vol. 1. New York: Scribner, Armstrong and Company, 1876.

Burton, C.M. *A Sketch of the Life of Antoine De La Mothe Cadillac*. Detroit, MI: Wilton-Smith Company, 1895.

Cady, Annie Cole. *The American Continent Before Columbus*. Vol. 2. Philadelphia: Gebbie and Company Publishers, 1894.

Chapelle, Howard I. *The History of American Sailing Ships*. New York: W.W. Norton & Company, 1935.

Clark, Thomas. *Naval History of the United States*. Vol. 1. Philadelphia: M. Carey, 1814.

Coolidge, A.J., and J.B. Mansfield. *A History and Description of New England*. Boston: Austin J. Coolidge, 1859.

Crawford, F. Marion. "Bar Harbor." *Scribner's* (September 1894).

Currier, Isabel. "The 'Edna Hoyt.'" *Down East* (June 1964).

Cutler, Carl. *Greyhounds of the Sea*. New York: Halcyon House, 1930.

Daily Boston Globe. "Last Five-Master Sails, Stampede in New York." August 25, 1934.

———. "*San Benito* Has Injured Man from Schooner On Board." December 23, 1928.

———. "Schooner 40 Days on Trip from Venezuela." October 10, 1929.

DeCosta, Benjamin F. *Ancient Norumbega*. Albany, NY: Joel Munsell's Sons, 1890.

Denison, John L. *An Illustrated History of the New World*. Norwich, CT: Henry Bill, 1868.

Diamond, Sigmund. "Norumbega: New England Xanadu." *American Neptune* 12 (1951).

Duncan, Roger F. *Coastal Maine: A Maritime History*. New York: W.W. Norton & Company, 1992.

Emery, John S. *The Sullivan Family of Sullivan, Maine, with Some Account of the Town*. Bangor, ME: John S. Emery, 1891.

Evening Independent [St. Petersburg, FL], January 2, 1945.

Fiske, John. *New France and New England*. Boston: Houghton, Mifflin & Company, 1902.

Foss, Harold. "From Shipmaster to Guano Merchant." *American Neptune* 24, no.1 (January 1964).

Frost, John. *Great Events in Modern History*. Boston: L.P. Crown & Company, 1855.

Gifford, John. *History of France*. Vol. 4. London: C. Loundes, Drury Lane, 1793.

Goodrich, S.G. *A Pictorial History of America.* Hartford, CT: E. Strong, 1844.

Hale, Richard Walden. *The Story of Bar Harbor.* New York: Ives Washburn, Inc., 1949.

Hall, Thomas. *The* T.W. Lawson*: The Fate of the World's Only Seven-Masted Schooner.* Charleston, SC: The History Press, 2006.

Hancock Historical Society. Letters.

Hancock, Maine, Town of. *A History of the Town of Hancock, 1828 to 1978.* Ellsworth, ME: Downeast Graphics, 1978.

Hart, Albert Bushnell. *American History Told by Contemporaries.* New York: Macmillan Company, 1900.

Hartwell, John J. "Prizes Taken by the Privateer Schooner Hannah and Molley, Agreen Crabtree, Master." Unpublished ms., 2001.

Hunt, Fred. "World's Largest Schooner Here." *Quincy Patriot Ledger*, September 4, 1936.

Jameson, J. Franklin. *Dictionary of United States History, 1492–1898.* Boston: Puritan Publishing Company, 1897.

———. *Early English and French Voyages, 1534–1608.* New York: Charles Scribner's Sons, 1906.

———. *Voyages of Samuel de Champlain, 1604–1618.* New York: Charles Scribner's Sons, 1907.

Lapham, William Berry. *Bar Harbor and Mount Desert Island.* New York: Press of Liberty, 1886.

"The Last Words and Dying Speech of Samuel L. Hadlock." *Chebacco* 2 (2005).

Lawrence [Kansas] *Journal-World*, January 2, 1945.

Lawton, Jordan, and Maddox Lawton. *The Island of Mt. Desert Register with the Cranberry Isles.* Auburn, ME: Lawton-Jordan Company, 1910.

Lewiston Daily Sun, December 11, 1929.

Literary Digest. "The Victory of Steam." January 11, 1908.

Long, Ralph Hamilton, Alice MacDonald Long and Mary H. Jones. "Hadlock Executed This Day." *History Journal of the Mount Desert Island Historical Society* (1998).

Marsh, Ron. "Tales of Wooden Ships, Iron Men, Told by Grizzled Yankee Skipper." *Montreal Gazette*, November 13, 1946.

Merriam, Charles. *Last of the Five-Masters.* New York: Claude Kendall, 1936.

Milner, Craig S., and Ralph W. Stanley. *Ralph Stanley: Tales of a Maine Boatbuilder.* Camden, ME: Down East Books, 2004.

Moore, Charles. *The Northwest Under Three Flags.* New York: Harper & Brothers Publishers, 1900.

Morison, Samuel Eliot. *The European Discovery of America.* New York: Oxford University Press, 1971.

———. *The Maritime History of Massachusetts*. Boston: Houghton Mifflin Company, 1921.

———. *The Story of Mount Desert Island.* Boston: Little, Brown and Company, 1960.

Morse, Jedidiah. *The American Universal Geography.* Boston: Isaiah Thomas and Ebenezer T. Andrews, 1802.

New England Historic & Genealogical Society. *The New England Historical & Genealogical Register*. Vol. 23. Boston: David Clapp & Sons, 1869.

New York Times. "Train Bringing $13,600,000." August 10, 1914.

———. "Women Rescued at Sea." December 21, 1901.

Parkman, Francis. *Count Frontenac*. Boston: Little, Brown and Company, 1913.

———. *A Half-Century of Conflict.* Boston: Little, Brown and Company, 1912.

———. *The Jesuits in North America.* Boston: Little, Brown and Company, 1902.

———. *Pioneers of France in the New World.* Boston: Little, Brown and Company, 1897.

Pember, John E. "City-Worn Youths Plead for Jobs on Last of 5-Masted Schooners." *Brooklyn Daily Eagle*, August 1934.

Robertson, William. *The History of the Discovery and Settlement of America.* New York: J&J Harper, 1831.

Schwieterman, Joseph. *When the Railroad Leaves Town.* Kirksville, MO: Truman State University Press, 2001.

Simpson, Dorothy. *The Maine Islands.* Philadelphia: J.B. Lippincott Company, 1960.

Snow, Edward Rowe. *Astounding Tales of the Sea.* New York: Dodd, Mead & Company, 1965.

Snow, Ralph Linwood, and Douglas K. Lee, captain. *A Shipyard in Maine: Percy & Small and the Great Schooners.* Gardiner, ME: Tilbury House Publishers, 1999.

Spokesman-Review, September 12, 1937.

Sprague, John Francis. *Sprague's Journal of Maine History.* Vol. 9. Dover, ME: John Francis Sprague, 1921.

Spruce, Christopher. "Discovery of Documents Sheds Light on Sunken Schooner." *Bangor Daily News*, October 11, 1979.

Street, George E. *Mount Desert, A History.* Boston: Houghton, Mifflin and Company, 1905.

Struik, Dirk J. *Yankee Science in the Making: Science and Engineering in New England from Colonial Times to the Civil War.* Mineola, NY: Dover Publications, 1992.

Sullivan, James. *The History of the District of Maine.* Boston: I. Thomas and E.T. Andrews, 1795.

Thwaites, Reuben Gold. *The Jesuit Relations and Allied Documents.* Vol. 3. Cleveland, OH: Burrows Brothers, 1896.

Tod, Giles M. *The Last Sail Down East.* Barre, MA: Barre Publishers, 1965.

Trott, Harlan. "Wanted: Five Real Sailors to Sail the *Edna Hoyt* Down to West Indies." *Christian Science Monitor*, November 14, 1935.

Varney, George J. *A Gazetteer of the State of Maine.* Boston: B.B. Russell, 1886.

Verrill, A Hyatt. *Romantic and Historic Maine.* New York: Dodd Mead & Company, 1935.

Wasson, George. *Sailing Days on the Penobscot.* New York: W.W. Norton and Company, 1949.

Wasson, Samuel. *A Survey of Hancock County, Maine.* Augusta, ME: Sprague, Owen & Nash, 1878.

Williamson, William D. *History of the State of Maine.* Vol. 1. Hallowell, ME: Glazier, Masters & Smith, 1839.

Windard, Jack. "Last Voyage of the Brig Homeward Bound." Unpublished ms., n.d.

———. "The Omnipotent Hand." Unpublished ms., n.d.

WEBSITES

"Allied Report on the Interrogations of Gimpel and Colepaugh." U.S. Navy Department. http://www.ibiblio.org/hyperwar/USN/rep/U-1230.

American Journeys Collection. "Hawkins Voyage of 1568." Wisconsin Historical Society Digital Library and Archives. http://americanjourneys.org.

Catholic Encyclopedia. "St. Ignatius Loyola." www.newadvent.org.

Centro Studi Storici Verrazzano. http://verrazzano.org.

Dictionary of Canadian Biography Online. http:// www.biographi.ca.

German U-boats of World War II. http://uboat.net/boats/u1230.htm.

Giovanni da Verrazzano. Letter to King Francis, 1524. http://www.nationalhumanitiescenter.org.

Jesuits of the New Orleans Province. www.norprov.org/spirituality/lifeofignatious.htm.

Juet, Robert. "The Third Voyage of Master Henrie Hudson, 1609." Wisconsin Historical Society Digital Library and Archives. www.wisconsinhistory.org/libraryarchives.

Penobscot Bay History Online. http://penobscotbayhistory.org.

Pilgrim Hall Museum. http://www.pilgrimhall.org/sailingoff.htm.

Sharp, David. "Skull Reveals North America's Earliest Autopsy." November 2006. www.livescience.com.

ABOUT THE AUTHOR

The author at the helm of the *Lewis R. French*, with the schooner *Victory Chimes* in the background. *Photo by Astrid Anderson.*

Ingrid Grenon was born in Maine, where she grew up in proximity to many treasures of previous centuries. Ingrid currently resides in southeastern Massachusetts, where she owns a small horse farm and is employed by the State Department of Developmental Disabilities. She holds a degree in psychology, as well as a degree in equestrian science, and also has a riding master's degree. In addition, Ingrid has a diploma in horseshoeing science from Oklahoma Farrier's College. She is also a published poet.

Ingrid is a member of the Boothbay Region Historical Society, the Somerset Historical Society, the Braintree Historical Society, the Mount Desert Island Historical Society, the Maine Maritime Museum, the Penobscot Marine Museum and the Maine Historical Society.

Other books by Ingrid Grenon

Simply This
Published by Antrim House Books, Simsbury, Connecticut
www.antrimhousebooks.com

Lost Maine Coastal Schooners: From Glory Days to Ghost Ships
Published by The History Press, Charleston, South Carolina
www.historypress.net